Islam

OPPOSING VIEWPOINTS®

Other Books of Related Interest

OPPOSING VIEWPOINTS SERIES

Culture Wars
The Ethics of World Religions
Extremist Groups
Human Rights
India and Pakistan
Iraq
The Middle East
National Security
Religion in America
Terrorism
The War on Terrorism

CURRENT CONTROVERSIES SERIES

Afghanistan
Iraq
The Middle East
Nationalism and Ethnic Conflict
The Terrorist Attack on America

AT ISSUE SERIES

Does the World Hate the United States?
Is America Helping Afghanistan?
Islamic Fundamentalism
*Is Military Action Justified Against Nations That Support
Terrorism?*
Should the United States Withdraw from Iraq?
U.S. Policy Toward Rogue Nations

Islam

OPPOSING VIEWPOINTS®

William Dudley, *Book Editor*

Bruce Glassman, *Vice President*
Bonnie Szumski, *Publisher*
Helen Cothran, *Managing Editor*

OPPOSING
VIEWPOINTS®
SERIES

GREENHAVEN
PRESS®

Brooks - Cork Library
Shelton State
Community College

THOMSON
━━━✶━━━ ™
GALE

San Diego • Detroit • New York • San Francisco • Cleveland
New Haven, Conn. • Waterville, Maine • London • Munich

For more information, contact
Greenhaven Press
27500 Drake Rd.
Farmington Hills, MI 48331-3535
Or you can visit our Internet site at http://www.gale.com

LIBRARY OF CONGRESS CATALOGING-IN-PUBLICATION DATA

Islam : opposing viewpoints / William Dudley, book editor.
    p. cm. — (Opposing viewpoints series)
    Includes bibliographical references and index.
    ISBN 0-7377-2238-X (lib. : alk. paper) — ISBN 0-7377-2239-8 (pbk. : alk. paper)
    1. Islam—Essence, genius, nature. 2. Islam—Relations—Christianity.
3. Christianity and other religions—Islam. 4. East and West. 5. Islam—Twenty-first century. I. Dudley, William, 1964– . II. Opposing viewpoints series (Unnumbered)
BP163.I7327   2004
297.2'7—dc22   2003067545

Printed in the United States of America

"Congress shall make
no law...abridging the
freedom of speech, or of
the press."

First Amendment to the U.S. Constitution

The basic foundation of our democracy is the First
Amendment guarantee of freedom of expression.
The Opposing Viewpoints Series is dedicated to the
concept of this basic freedom and the idea that it is
more important to practice it than to enshrine it.

Contents

Why Consider Opposing Viewpoints?

"The only way in which a human being can make some approach to knowing the whole of a subject is by hearing what can be said about it by persons of every variety of opinion and studying all modes in which it can be looked at by every character of mind. No wise man ever acquired his wisdom in any mode but this."

John Stuart Mill

In our media-intensive culture it is not difficult to find differing opinions. Thousands of newspapers and magazines and dozens of radio and television talk shows resound with differing points of view. The difficulty lies in deciding which opinion to agree with and which "experts" seem the most credible. The more inundated we become with differing opinions and claims, the more essential it is to hone critical reading and thinking skills to evaluate these ideas. Opposing Viewpoints books address this problem directly by presenting stimulating debates that can be used to enhance and teach these skills. The varied opinions contained in each book examine many different aspects of a single issue. While examining these conveniently edited opposing views, readers can develop critical thinking skills such as the ability to compare and contrast authors' credibility, facts, argumentation styles, use of persuasive techniques, and other stylistic tools. In short, the Opposing Viewpoints Series is an ideal way to attain the higher-level thinking and reading skills so essential in a culture of diverse and contradictory opinions.

In addition to providing a tool for critical thinking, Opposing Viewpoints books challenge readers to question their own strongly held opinions and assumptions. Most people form their opinions on the basis of upbringing, peer pressure, and personal, cultural, or professional bias. By reading carefully balanced opposing views, readers must directly confront new ideas as well as the opinions of those with whom they disagree. This is not to simplistically argue that

9

everyone who reads opposing views will—or should—change his or her opinion. Instead, the series enhances readers' understanding of their own views by encouraging confrontation with opposing ideas. Careful examination of others' views can lead to the readers' understanding of the logical inconsistencies in their own opinions, perspective on why they hold an opinion, and the consideration of the possibility that their opinion requires further evaluation.

Evaluating Other Opinions

To ensure that this type of examination occurs, Opposing Viewpoints books present all types of opinions. Prominent spokespeople on different sides of each issue as well as well-known professionals from many disciplines challenge the reader. An additional goal of the series is to provide a forum for other, less known, or even unpopular viewpoints. The opinion of an ordinary person who has had to make the decision to cut off life support from a terminally ill relative, for example, may be just as valuable and provide just as much insight as a medical ethicist's professional opinion. The editors have two additional purposes in including these less known views. One, the editors encourage readers to respect others' opinions—even when not enhanced by professional credibility. It is only by reading or listening to and objectively evaluating others' ideas that one can determine whether they are worthy of consideration. Two, the inclusion of such viewpoints encourages the important critical thinking skill of objectively evaluating an author's credentials and bias. This evaluation will illuminate an author's reasons for taking a particular stance on an issue and will aid in readers' evaluation of the author's ideas.

It is our hope that these books will give readers a deeper understanding of the issues debated and an appreciation of the complexity of even seemingly simple issues when good and honest people disagree. This awareness is particularly important in a democratic society such as ours in which people enter into public debate to determine the common good. Those with whom one disagrees should not be regarded as enemies but rather as people whose views deserve careful examination and may shed light on one's own.

Thomas Jefferson once said that "difference of opinion leads to inquiry, and inquiry to truth." Jefferson, a broadly educated man, argued that "if a nation expects to be ignorant and free . . . it expects what never was and never will be." As individuals and as a nation, it is imperative that we consider the opinions of others and examine them with skill and discernment. The Opposing Viewpoints Series is intended to help readers achieve this goal.

David L. Bender and Bruno Leone,
Founders

Greenhaven Press anthologies primarily consist of previously published material taken from a variety of sources, including periodicals, books, scholarly journals, newspapers, government documents, and position papers from private and public organizations. These original sources are often edited for length and to ensure their accessibility for a young adult audience. The anthology editors also change the original titles of these works in order to clearly present the main thesis of each viewpoint and to explicitly indicate the opinion presented in the viewpoint. These alterations are made in consideration of both the reading and comprehension levels of a young adult audience. Every effort is made to ensure that Greenhaven Press accurately reflects the original intent of the authors included in this anthology.

Introduction

*"Only when the 'war on terrorism' becomes 'war on
militant Islam' can the war actually be won."*

—Daniel Pipes

*"Islam—as a religion, culture, and society—most
emphatically is not an enemy of the West."*

—Antony T. Sullivan

Karen Armstrong, author of several books on religion, tells
the story of trying in the early 1990s to find a publisher for
her book *A History of God*, a study of the theological thought
of Judaism, Christianity, and Islam. She writes that one
American publisher was interested in the book but asked her
to shorten or remove all the chapters dealing with Islam because American readers were not interested in "all this Muslim theology." Americans, Armstrong recounted, "tended to
regard the Muslim world as irredeemably religious and
therefore barbarous and dangerous, or to dismiss Islam as an
archaic irrelevance"—this despite the fact that Islam was one
of the world's great religions with more than a billion adherents (including several million in the United States).
Armstrong's findings that Americans were disinterested in
Islam were echoed in a 1993 *Time* magazine poll that revealed that almost two-thirds of Americans, when asked their
impression of Islam, answered "not aware" or "don't know."

A single traumatic event changed all this. After the event,
bookstores suddenly reported selling out copies of the Koran, the sacred text of Islam, as well as other books about Islam. Librarians reported a similar spike in patrons seeking
information about Islam. Enrollment in college classes on
Islam, the Middle East, and Arabic skyrocketed. The news
media became filled with programs and articles discussing
jihad and other terms previously unfamiliar to most Americans. Mosques suddenly hosted open houses, welcoming
non-Muslims to come and learn about Islam; even the president of the United States took advantage of this opportunity by visting the Islamic Center of Washington, D.C.

The catalytic event that sparked all this public interest in Islam was, of course, the September 11, 2001, terrorist attacks. Nineteen self-proclaimed Muslim fanatics hijacked four commercial airliners, flying two of them into the World Trade Center towers in New York City and one into the Pentagon in Washington, D.C.; the fourth plane crashed in a field in Pennsylvania. All told, three thousand people from eighty different nations perished in the attacks. While it was not the first terrorist event on U.S. soil involving Muslims (radical Islamists had tried to bomb the World Trade Center in 1993), the shocking scope of the September 11 attack raised questions in the minds of many Americans about whether Islam, the world's fastest-growing religion, constituted a threat to American security.

Islam is the newest of the three monotheistic religions that originated in roughly the same part of the world, following Judaism and Christianity. It was founded by Muhammad, a merchant from the Arab town of Mecca, in the 600s. Muslims believe that Muhammad acted as a "transmitter" for the words of God (Allah), which were collected and became the Koran. Islam quickly spread from Arabia, and Muslims today come from many different linguistic and cultural backgrounds. All observant Muslims share certain beliefs, including the "Five Pillars" of Islam. These pillars mandate the profession of faith that there is only one true God (Allah) and that Muhammad was God's messenger, the practice of praying five times a day while facing Mecca, the giving of charity to the poor, the observance of a fast during the holy month of Ramadan, and (for those who can afford it), a pilgrimmage to holy sites in Mecca. Some Muslims add a "sixth pillar"—*jihad*, which literally means "struggle" and is sometimes translated as "holy war." Letters left behind by the September 11 terrorists indicated that they believed that their acts were part of a jihad against a country they deemed an enemy of Islam.

Interestingly, however, the Arabic word *Islam* means "submission" (to the will of Allah) and shares the same root as the Arabic word for peace. President George W. Bush, during his September visit to the Islamic Center as well as on other occasions, is among those who have asserted that Islam is a religion of peace and that the September 11 terrorists did not truly represent the religion. He said, "These acts of violence against innocents violate the fundamental tenets of the Islamic faith, and it's important for my fellow Americans to understand that. . . . The face of terror is not the true faith of Islam. That's not what Islam is all about. Islam is peace." Bush's announcements were echoed by several American Muslim organizations, including the International Institute on Islamic Thought (IIIT). In a flyer produced after the attacks, the IIIT asserted that "terrorism goes against every principle in Islam" and denied that the September 11 terrorists were engaged in jihad. Jihad should not be translated simply as "holy war," the IIIT argued, but should be viewed as an "Islamic concept that includes struggle against evil inclinations against oneself, struggle to improve the quality of life in society, struggle in the battle for self-defense or fighting against tyranny and oppression." The IIIT and others who assert the peaceful nature of Islam cite the same verse in the Koran: "Whoever killed a human being, except as a punishment for murder or villainy in the land, shall be looked upon as though he had killed all mankind."

Not everyone agrees with the interpretations of jihad provided by Bush and the IIIT, however. Some observers argue that war or struggle against non-Islamic nations has historically been a central component of the Islamic religion, and that Islam continues to motivate terrorists. Scholar and author Robert Spencer asserts that while some Muslims speak out against terrorism and violence, the radical views of the September 11 terrorists are not necessarily a fringe or extremist part of Islam but are a natural outgrowth of fundamental teachings found in the Koran and other central Islamic writings. He argues, "Radical Muslims use the Qur'an [Koran] and other core Islamic teachings to justify their [violent] actions, and their exegesis is compelling enough to win over large numbers of radicals." Spencer adds: "Terrorism is not universally accepted in the Islamic world, but . . . terrorist groups [are] rallying under the banner of jihad in all corners of the globe today." Some verses in the Koran seem to support this view, including one urging Muslims to "make war on the unbelievers and the hypocrites." Some Muslim religious leaders have argued that this verse can justify violence and warfare "as a punishment for murder or villainy in the land."

The debate over the connection between Islam, violence, and terrorism continues to rage long after the events of September 11, 2001. The controversy is one of several addressed in *Islam: Opposing Viewpoints*. An array of scholars, political analysts, Islamic activists, and others offer contrasting views about Islam in the following chapters: Are the Values of Islam and the West in Conflict? Does Islam Promote Terrorism and Violence? What Is the Status of Women Under Islam? How Will Islam's Future Be Shaped? The authors in this anthology examine conflicting perceptions of Islam and its values, and how these values affect Muslim societies and the West in the post–September 11 era.

CHAPTER 1

Are the Values of Islam and the West in Conflict?

Chapter Preface

In his 1996 book *The Clash of Civilizations and the Remaking of the World Order*, Harvard University political scientist Samuel P. Huntington posits that the basic sources of conflict in today's world have cultural rather than political or economic roots. He argues that "the fault lines between civilizations will be the battle lines of the future." He goes on to identify Islam and the West as "highly integrated civilizations" that will likely clash in the future. Conflict between Islam and the West was once a contest between two competing religions—Islam and Christianity. However, today frictions between them have more to do with the contrast between Islam (with its many rules and traditions governing law, society, and daily life) and secular Western values such as representative democracy, separation of religion and politics, and market capitalism. Efforts to encourage the spread of such Western values in Islamic countries may be unsuccessful, Huntington and others argue, and could lead to open conflict. "The dangerous clashes of the future," Huntington writes, "are likely to arise from the interaction of Western arrogance [and] Islamic intolerance."

Not everyone agrees with Huntington's analysis of an inherent conflict between Islam and the West, however. For one thing, scholars Graham E. Fuller and Ian O. Lesser argue, Islam encompasses diverse beliefs and cultures and cannot "be treated as a single, cohesive, coherent . . . monolithic entity." Muslim scholar and former president of Indonesia Abdurrahman Wahid has called the "clash of civilizations" theory flawed and based on double standards; he contends that any Muslim violence is interpreted as a "clash" with the West, while other violence within Western societies is ignored. "The fact is that hundreds of thousands of Muslims study in Western [educational] institutions—they take from the West, and the West takes from us. To see the relationship as a confrontation between the two [cultures] is a mistake," Wahid asserts. "Of course, we do have differences, but differences do not mean enmity and clashes."

The September 11, 2001, terrorist attacks against the United States, carried out by professed Muslims, and America's subsequent attacks against Afghanistan and Iraq have raised more questions over whether a general war between Islam and the West is taking place. Huntington's idea of a "clash of civilizations" is one of several theories and ideas regarding Islam and the West that are examined in this chapter.

"Most of what western society claims as its own highest ideals are deeply rooted in Islamic tradition."

Islam Is Compatible with Western Values

Hamza Yusuf

Hamza Yusuf, an American who converted to Islam in 1977 and subsequently traveled to the Middle East and Africa to study Arabic and Islam, is director of the Zaytouna Institute, a California-based school dedicated to the revival of the traditional teaching methods and sciences of Islam. In the following viewpoint he argues that Western criticisms of Islam are based on ignorance and prejudice. In fact, he contends, Islam is compatible with core Western values. He rejects the notion of an inevitable "clash" between Islamic and Western societies.

As you read, consider the following questions:
1. What responses does Yusuf make to complaints about the role of women in Islam?
2. What comparison does the author make between Western attitudes toward Muslims and Jews?
3. Why does Yusuf reject the "clash of civilizations" thesis?

When a Welsh resistance leader was captured and brought before the emperor in Rome, he said: "Because you desire to conquer the world, it does not necessarily follow that the world desires to be conquered by you." Today one could offer an echo of this sentiment to western liberals: "Because you wish your values to prevail throughout the world, it does not always follow that the world wishes to adopt them." The imperial voice is based on ignorance of the rich traditions of other civilisations, and on an undue optimism about what the west is doing to the world politically, economically and environmentally.

The entrenched beliefs many westerners profess about Islam often reveal more about the west than they do about Islam or Muslims. The Ottomans were history's longest-lasting major dynasty;[1] their durability must have had some relation to their ability to rule a multi-faith empire at a time when Europe was busily hanging, drawing and quartering different varieties of Christian believer.

Islam and Women

Today Islam is said to be less, not more, tolerant than the west, and we need to ask which, precisely, are the "western" values with which Islam is so incompatible? Some believe Islam's attitude towards women is the source of the Muslim "problem." Westerners need to look to their own attitudes here and recognise that only very recently have patriarchal structures begun to erode in the west.

The Islamic tradition does show some areas of apparent incompatibility with the goals of women in the west, and Muslims have a long way to go in their attitudes towards women. But blaming the religion is again to express an ignorance both of the religion and of the historical struggle for equality of women in Muslim societies.

A careful reading of modern female theologians of Islam would cause western women to be impressed by legal injunctions more than 1,000 years old that, for instance, grant women legal rights to domestic help at the expense of their

1. The Ottoman Empire ruled much of the Muslim world and parts of Europe from the 1400s to 1918.

husbands. Three of the four Sunni schools consider domestic chores outside the scope of a woman's legal responsibilities toward her husband. Contrast that with US polls showing that working women still do 80% of domestic chores.

Westerners, in their advocacy of global conformism, often speak of "progress" and the rejection of the not-too-distant feudal past, and are less likely to reveal their unease about corporate hegemony and the real human implications of globalisation.

Islam Is Part of the West

Islam—as a religion, culture and society—most emphatically is not an enemy of the West.

Those who argue the contrary slander not only the third and last of the three great Abrahamic revelations but make all too likely the outbreak of either a religious war pitting Christianity (and perhaps Judaism) against Islam or a war of civilizations pitting the West against the entire Muslim world. And be assured: Any wars of religion or civilization will not be wars that the West—or the United States—will win. . . .

Not only is Islam not an enemy of the West, but it, like Judaism, is part of the larger civilizational ecumene that we in the contemporary West know—or ought to. In fact, the West stops at the Indus, not at the Dardanelles. Today, Islam is part and parcel of the West, just as the West is part and parcel of Islam.

Antony T. Sullivan, *Insight on the News*, November 5, 2001.

Neither are the missionaries of western values willing to consider why Europe, the heart of the west, should have generated two world wars which killed more civilians than all the wars of the previous 20 centuries. As Muslims point out, we are asked to call them "world wars" despite their reality as western wars, which targeted civilians with weapons of mass destruction at a time when Islam was largely at peace.

We Muslims are unpersuaded by many triumphalist claims made for the west, but are happy with its core values. As a westerner, the child of civil rights and anti-war activists, I embraced Islam not in abandonment of my core values, drawn almost entirely from the progressive tradition, but as an affirmation of them. I have since studied Islamic law for

10 years with traditionally trained scholars, and while some particulars in medieval legal texts have troubled me, never have the universals come into conflict with anything my progressive Californian mother taught me. Instead, I have marvelled at how most of what western society claims as its own highest ideals are deeply rooted in Islamic tradition.

Islam and Anti-Semitism

The chauvinism apparent among some westerners is typically triggered by Islamic extremism. Few take the trouble to notice that mainstream Islam dislikes the extremists as much as the west does. What I fear is that an excuse has been provided to supply some westerners with a replacement for their older habit of anti-semitism. The shift is not such a difficult one. Arabs, after all, are semites, and the Arabian prophet's teaching is closer in its theology and law to Judaism than it is to Christianity. We Muslims in the west, like Jews before us, grapple with the same issues that Jews of the past did: integration or isolation, tradition or reform, intermarriage or intra-marriage.

Muslims who yearn for an ideal Islamic state are in some ways reflecting the old aspirations of the Diaspora Jews for a homeland where they would be free to be different. Muslims, like Jews, often dress differently; we cannot eat some of the food of the host countries. Like the Jews of the past, we are now seen as parasites on the social body, burdened with a uniform and unreformable law, contributing little, scheming in ghettoes, and obscurely indifferent to personal hygiene.

Cartoons of Arabs seem little different to the caricatures of Jews in German newspapers of the Nazi period. In the 1930s, such images ensured that few found the courage to speak out about the possible consequences of such a demonisation, just as few today are really thinking about the anti-Muslim rhetoric of the extreme-right parties across Europe. Muslims in general, and Arabs especially, have become the new "other."

No Clash of Civilisations

When I met President [George W.] Bush last year [2001], I gave him two books. One was *The Essential Koran*, translated by Thomas Cleary. The second was another translation by Cleary, *Thunder in the Sky: Secrets of the Acquisition and Use of Power.* Written by an ancient Chinese sage, it reflects the universal values of another great people.

I did this because, as an American, rooted in the best of western tradition, and a Muslim convert who finds much of profundity in Chinese philosophy, I believe the "Huntington thesis" that these three great civilisations must inevitably clash is a lie. Each civilisation speaks with many voices; the best of them find much in common. Not only can our civilisations co-exist in our respective parts of the world, they can co-exist in the individual heart, as they do in mine. We can enrich each other if we choose to embrace our essential humanity; we can destroy the world if we choose to stress our differences.

| "*We might reasonably wonder whether our attempts to live side by side with Islam are doomed to failure.*"

Islam Is Not Compatible with Western Values

Roger Scruton

Roger Scruton is a conservative English writer and philosopher who has written numerous books, including *The West and the Rest: Globalization and the Terrorist Threat*. In the following viewpoint he argues that Islam promotes values that conflict with those of Western societies. He contrasts Islam with Christianity, arguing that Western societies under Christianity have developed the idea that government is a human endeavor that should be kept apart from religion. Islam, by contrast, places all political authority in the writings of the Koran, its holy book. Islam also dictates that all people should submit to Islamic teachings. The result, Scruton concludes, is that many Muslims have rejected modernity and believe that Islam is not just incompatible with, but is fundamentally opposed to, the basic values of Western nations.

As you read, consider the following questions:

1. What comment does Scruton make about the organizational structure of Islam?
2. How did Islam spread throughout the Middle East and other areas, according to the author?
3. Why does Scruton believe that Islam is not a religion of peace?

Roger Scruton, "Religion of Peace? Islam, Without the Comforting Cliches," *National Review*, vol. 24, December 31, 2002. Copyright © 2002 by National Review, Inc., 215 Lexington Ave., New York, NY 10016. Reproduced by permission.

Western societies—when faced with immigrants who adhere to traditional faiths and customs, and who maintain a suspicion-laden distance between themselves and the surrounding civil order—tend to respond with overtures of friendship. The message relayed to the new communities that have sought protection in the West is one of tolerance and understanding. By showing that we are no threat to them, we hope to ensure that they will be no threat to us. This strategy has worked with Hindus and Jews and the many sects of migrating Christians. But will it work with Muslims? When from the pulpits of the mosques that have been built in our major cities there sounds the call to jihad [holy war] against the infidel, along with exultant cries of triumph over the recent terrorist atrocities, we might reasonably wonder whether our attempts to live side by side with Islam are doomed to failure.

Its official advocates insist that Islam is a religion of peace—after all, that is the meaning of the word (or, at least, one of its meanings). But the peculiar thing about Islam is that its official advocates have no authority to speak for it. Although each sect has its mosques, there is no such institution as "The Mosque," to set beside the various Christian churches. Nor is there any human institution whose role is to confer "holy orders" on its members. Muslims who have religious authority—the 'ulama ("those with knowledge")—possess it directly from God. And those who take on the function of the imam ("the one who stands in front"), so leading the congregation in prayer, are often self-appointed to this role. Islam lacks the chain of human accountability that stems from the corporate personality of an organized church. Thus the only way to settle the question whether Islam is or is not a religion of peace is to study the actions of individual Muslims, and the text from which their religion derives.

The Koran

The Koran is considered the final authority on all matters it touches upon—and that means just about all matters that impinge on the lives of ordinary mortals. Its style is exhortatory, and its mood imperative. It resounds with threats and imprecations and, for all its many passages of lyrical beauty, it is the biggest joke-free zone in literature. It occupies the space reserved in the human psyche for obedience, and leaves no room for any merely human jurisdiction. The Koranic conception of law as holy law, pointing the unique way to salvation and applying to every area of human life, therefore involves a confiscation of the political. Those matters which, in Western societies, are resolved by negotiation, compromise, and the laborious work of offices and committees are the object of immovable and eternal decrees. The rules are either laid down explicitly in the holy book or discerned there by some religious figurehead—whose authority, however, can always be questioned by some rival imam or jurist, since the shari'a (holy law) recognizes no office or institution as endowed with any independent lawmaking power. The shari'a, moreover, is addressed to the faithful, wherever and with whomsoever they find themselves; it does not merely bind Muslims but isolates them from the secular society by which they are surrounded. In any crisis secular law will count for nothing, since the law of God eclipses it.

Islamic Law Prohibits Western Freedoms

In most countries where Islamic law dominates there is practically no freedom of religion (not to mention freedom of speech or the press). In most Islamic countries, including so-called moderate Islamic states such as Saudi Arabia, it is a crime to build a Christian church, Jewish synagogue, Hindu temple or any other non-Muslim house of worship. In contrast, there are about 3,000 mosques in the U.S., with new ones being built every week.

Muslims are free to worship Allah in the U.S., but Christians are not free to worship Jesus in most Muslim countries.

Franklin Graham, *Wall Street Journal*, December 9, 2001.

The contrast with Christianity is instructive. St. Paul, who turned the ascetic and self-denying religion of Christ into an organized form of worship, was a Roman citizen, versed in the law, who shaped the early Church through the legal idea of the universitas or corporation. The Pauline Church was designed not as a sovereign body, but as a universal citizen, entitled to the protection of the secular and imperial powers but with no claim to displace those powers as the source of legal order. This corresponds to Christ's own vision in the parable of the tribute money: "Render therefore to Caesar the things that are Caesar's; and unto God the things that are God's." The Church has therefore tended to recognize the business of governing human society as a human business, and the Christian as both a servant of God and a citizen of the secular order. It is a distinctive Christian achievement to propose secular government as a religious duty, and religious toleration as an avenue to God. The Enlightenment conception of the citizen, as joined in a free social contract with his neighbors under a tolerant and secular rule of law, derives directly from the Christian legacy.

This contrasts radically with the vision set before us in the Koran, according to which sovereignty rests with God and his Prophet, and legal order is founded in divine command. True law is holy law, whose precepts derive from the four sources of Islamic legal thought: the Koran, the Sunna (customs authorized by the Prophet), qiyas ("analogy"), and ijma' ("consensus"). These are the sources to which the classical jurists referred when giving judgment, and none of them acknowledge any lawmaking institution of merely human provenance. They are the means for discerning God's will, and so attaining the posture of submission (the literal meaning of Islam).

Conquest and Decline

When Islam first spread across the Middle East and the Southern Mediterranean, it was not by preaching and conversion in the Christian manner, but by conquest. The conquered peoples were given the choice: believe or die. Exceptions were made for the "people of the Book" (Christians, Jews, and Zoroastrians), who could enjoy the subordinate status of dhimmi—i.e., being protected by treaty. But the treaty offered no right to worship, and forbade all attempts to proselytize. Other religions existed within the dar al-islam on sufferance, and religious toleration was regarded as a regrettable expedient rather than a political virtue.

Under the Ottoman Empire, Islam steadily lost both its belligerent attitude to other faiths and its ability to maintain itself through religious law. In the 19th century the Ottoman sultans began to borrow laws, institutions, and secular customs from the West, so that when the empire collapsed after World War I, its center was able to jettison the perimeter and reshape itself as a modern secular state on the Western model. Thus was born modern Turkey, the creation of Kemal Ataturk, and the one durable democracy in the Muslim world. Turkey endures as a democracy because it has secularized its institutions and excluded the clergy from power. In no sense, however, can it be seen as the product of a Muslim "Enlightenment," equivalent to the Enlightenment that transformed the legal and political order of Europe. Turkey is a deliberately Westernized state.

Elsewhere in the Islamic world the democratic idea has not taken root—not because people have rejected it, but because their culture, habits, and institutions make no room for it. Secular government is kept in place by dictatorship, or by ruthless expedients that confer no legitimacy but only power on those who deploy them. In the Middle East, dictatorships designed to retain power in the hands of a single person, a single family, or a single dominant tribe exist side by side with a near-universal nostalgia for another and purer form of government, in which the holy law delivered to the Prophet will bring lasting peace and justice under the rule of God.

An Immovable Nostalgia

It has often been said that Islam has turned its back on modernity, which it cannot encompass through its law and doctrine. And to some extent this is true, the effects of Westernizers and legal reformers notwithstanding. Much more important, however, is the intense longing for that original and pure community once promised by the Prophet but betrayed repeatedly by his worldly successors and followers. Like every form of nostalgia, this longing involves a turning away from reality, a refusal to accommodate or even to perceive the facts that might undermine it, and an endlessly renewable anger against the Other who refuses to share in the collective dream. This is the mood that inspires the Muslim Brotherhood in Egypt, the Wahhabi sect in Saudi Arabia, and the Shi'ite revival of Ayatollah Khomeini [in Iran]. And it is the mood that animates the Islamist terrorists.

Rulers of Islamic states are aware of the danger posed by this immovable nostalgia. They know that it recognizes no loyalty to dynasty, territory, or secular law, but only to God and His promises. Hence they ruthlessly suppress the Islamist movements in their midst—as Hafez al-Assad suppressed the Muslim Brotherhood in the town of Hama in Syria, leaving 10,000 dead and a great medieval town in ruins. Similar measures have been taken in Egypt, Iraq, Tunisia, Algeria, and Saudi Arabia. But the threat is always there, and the measures must always be renewed.

It is in the light of such facts that we should assess the claim that Islam is a religion of peace. Long periods of peace have indeed been enjoyed in the heartlands of Islam, and there are good historical reasons for believing that Muslim communities can live at peace with their Christian, Jewish, or Zoroastrian neighbors. But these periods of peace are periods of lethargy, laxity, and decline. Muslim revivals, when they occur, take a belligerent form. The message that inspires them is not, like the Christian message, one of renunciation and forgiveness, but one of exhortation and triumph. No Christian sect poses the kind of threat to government that the Muslim Brotherhood has posed in Egypt and Syria. And even if we disapprove of the ruthless methods used to suppress the Brotherhood, this very ruthlessness is an indication of the danger.

How Western and Islamic Societies Handle Dissent

Western societies tolerate and even welcome dissent, and our disputes are resolved through compromise and dialogue. Thanks to our Christian legacy we see political action not as a means to achieve the kingdom of God on earth, but as a way of maintaining equilibrium between people who share a territory but who may not share a religion, and whose conflicts can be resolved through a common national loyalty and a common territorial law. None of that is accepted by the Islamists. By offering them a home we free them from the chains in which the tyrants of the Middle East try to bind them. But we do not free them from the pathological hatred of our sinful world, nor from the desire to make the ultimate sacrifice in the jihad against it. Hence while we offer them a home, what they receive is a "base"—the literal meaning of al-qa'eda.[1]

That is why we should regard our current situation as dangerous. We are not dealing with ordinary criminals of the IRA [Irish Republican Army] variety, whose sentimental nationalism conceals a self-centered search for gangland profits and power. We are dealing with people in the grip of religious zeal, for whom everything is permitted that leads toward their goal, and whose goal is destruction. The weapons that we use against ordinary criminals are therefore ineffective against the Islamists. In order to protect ourselves against them we must take pre-emptive measures. This does not mean that we should ghettoize or persecute our Muslim communities. But we must be prepared to break up Islamist cells, and to prevent them from obtaining the arms and the knowledge that would enable them to engage in the longed-for jihad. And we shouldn't deceive ourselves. This jihad really is longed for, and if we are not vigilant, it really will occur.

1. Al-Qaeda is the terrorist group responsible for the September 11, 2001, terrorist attacks.

"The Islamic world has always been marked by the centralization of theocracy."

Islam Presents an Obstacle to Democracy

Robert Spencer

Robert Spencer is the author of *Islam Unveiled: Disturbing Questions About the World's Fastest-Growing Faith*, from which the following viewpoint is excerpted. In it he considers what might happen in the United States if Muslims become the majority population. He contends that America would be fundamentally changed because Islamic values are foreign to American and Western concepts of democracy. In contrast to the practice of most democracies, which separate religious and political affairs, Islam prescribes a comprehensive system of law and government in which all aspects of life are subject to religious oversight. Islam and democracy may be ultimately incompatible, Spencer concludes.

As you read, consider the following questions:
1. What attempts in history have been made to establish democracy in an Islamic context, according to Spencer?
2. How did the early history of Islam compare with that of Christianity, according to the author?
3. What five major types of Muslim societies exist, according to Spencer?

"**A**merica counts millions of Muslims amongst our citizens," said President George W. Bush in the Islamic Center of Washington, D.C., just six days after terrorist attacks destroyed the World Trade Center and a portion of the Pentagon [on September 11, 2001].

> Muslims make an incredibly valuable contribution to our country. Muslims are doctors, lawyers, law professors, members of the military, entrepreneurs, shopkeepers, moms and dads. . . . This is a great country. It's a great country because we share the same values of respect and dignity and human worth. And it is my honor to be meeting with leaders who feel just the same way I do. They're outraged, they're sad. They love America just as much as I do.

No doubt this is true. A Muslim businessman I know—a kind and thoughtful man—proudly (or prudently) sported an "I love the USA" sweatshirt in the weeks following September 11. There is no indication that he received any flak for this at the mosque on Friday.

A Thought Experiment

But consider a thought experiment: what would happen if these Muslim citizens became a majority in the United States? Although such a possibility is several generations from having the chance to become an actuality, this is more than just idle speculation: Islamic advocates say that theirs is the fastest-growing religion in the world, and it is expanding very quickly in the United States as well. Muslim populations are growing rapidly in Western Europe, and practicing Muslims will shortly outnumber practicing Anglicans in Great Britain, the home of Anglicanism.

Americans who have thought about Muslim demographics are not alarmed. After all, even if the Islamic population continues to increase at a rapid clip, it isn't likely to alter the flow of public discourse. Moreover, the idea of the separation of church and state is well established in the United States. Christians who have attempted to influence political debate in recent decades have learned through hard experience that they must avoid all appearance of trying to "legislate morality." A secular American republic with a Muslim majority would continue as before, no?

It might. There have been notable attempts to establish

democracy in an Islamic context. The great opponent of the Wahhabis, the Egyptian modernist Muhammad Abduh (1849–1905), tried to recast traditional Islamic categories to reflect those of the modern West:

> Arguing that Islam was not incompatible with the basics of Western thought, Abdu[h] interpreted the Islamic concept of shura (consultation) as parliamentary democracy, ijma (consensus) as public opinion, and maslah (choosing that ruling or interpretation of the Sharia from which greatest good will ensue) as utilitarianism.[1]

But this doesn't mean that Abduh would have applauded Thomas Jefferson's "wall of separation between church and state." His vision of parliamentary democracy was thoroughly Islamic. His influential disciple Muhammad Rashid Rida (1865–1935) emphasized that "the affairs of the Islamic state must be conducted within the framework of a constitution that is inspired by the Quran, the Hadith and the experiences of the Rightly Guided Caliphs [the leaders of the Muslim community right after the time of Muhammad]."[2]

The Tunisian Muslim journalist and theorist Mohamed Elhachmi Hamdi concurs: "The heart of the matter is that no Islamic state can be legitimate in the eyes of its subjects without obeying the main teachings of the shari'a."

[Writer] V.S. Naipaul explains, "No religion is more worldly than Islam. In spite of its political incapacity, no religion keeps men's eyes more fixed on the way the world is run." He cites a typical article from the *Tehran Times*, published in the early days of Khomeini's revolution:[3] "Politics is combined with religion in Islam." The writer of the article recommends that Iran and Pakistan join together in a political partnership "with reformation and adaptation to present needs in full conformity with the holy Koran and Sunnah." He concludes that "Iran and Pakistan with a clarity of purpose and sincere cooperation can establish the truth that Islam is a complete way of life."

Mohamed Elhachmi Hamdi insists that "Islam should be the main frame of reference for the constitution and laws of

1. Passage from Dilip Hiro, *Holy Wars: The Rise of Islamic Fundamentalism*, 1989. 2. Hiro, *Holy Wars*. 3. Ayatollah Khomeini led a revolution that established an Islamic government in Iran in 1979.

predominantly Muslim countries." According to journalist Dinesh D'Souza, the influential Muslim radical Sayyid Qutb (1906–1966) argued that in an ideal polity, "it is God and not man who rules. God is the source of all authority, including legitimate political authority. Virtue, not freedom, is the highest value. Therefore God's laws, not man's, should govern the society." Likewise the Ayatollah Khomeini in Iran rejected rule "based on the approval of laws in accordance with the opinion of the majority." Only Allah can make laws. In practice, of course, that makes for an autocracy under the Sharia, or pressure for such a political arrangement, wherever Muslims form a majority.

Not only is the Sharia sufficient in itself for the governing of society; it extends to "the totality of religious, political, social, domestic and private life" [according to religion scholar Tore Kjeilen]. It governs personal conduct as well as the ordering of society. Islam has always prided itself on rejecting the distinction between that which is rendered unto Caesar and that which is rendered unto God. Muhammad, after all, was a political leader as well as a religious one. All aspects of life in an Islamic state are subject to religious authority. Everything is rendered unto Allah.

An Empire from the Beginning

Muslims count the beginning of the Islamic era not from Muhammad's birth or even from the time of his first revelation. Instead, they date it from the Hegira, when Muhammad left Mecca for Medina to become for the first time, if only on a small scale at that point, head of state and commander of armed forces at once.

Muslims never shared the experience of early Christians, of being a persecuted minority within a hostile regime. (Some would say they tasted this during the period of Western colonialism, but even then they remained the majority in their societies, and the colonial governments generally dared not overtly confront Islam.) State power and religious power were fused in Islam from its inception, centering on the caliph as the leader chosen by Allah for his people. Even though the caliphate is no more since the fall of the Ottoman Empire in 1918 (although fanatical Muslims, including Osama bin Laden [who was responsible for orchestrating the September 11 attacks], call for its restoration), the Islamic world has always been marked by the centralization of theocracy.

Democracy and God's Will

If by democracy one means an occasional election with a limited choice of candidates who cannot speak freely and no voting for the most powerful position—then, sure, Islamism (or fundamentalist Islam, as it sometimes is called) has no problems with democracy. But if the term refers to a system in which citizens have those rights (freedom of speech, the rule of law, minority rights, an independent judiciary) needed to make free and intelligent decisions, that they have a real choice of candidates and that they can vote for the top leader— then, no, Islamism is resoundingly not democratic.

Islamists believe in divine sovereignty and express a frank and deep disdain for popular sovereignty, which happens to be the key idea behind democracy. Instead, they hold that Muslims need nothing more than Islamic law (the Shariah) as applied by an Islamist ruler: "A free man is one who obeys Allah's rules and orders and worships God alone." How the ruler gets to power has to do with God's will, not man's.

Daniel Pipes, *Insight on the News*, August 14, 2000.

The Ayatollah Khomeini remarked, "What is the good of us [i.e., the mullahs] asking for the hand of a thief to be severed or an adulteress to be stoned to death when all we can do is recommend such punishments, having no power to implement them?" This is why Islam resists democracy. The Qur'an presents the clear and absolute law of Allah (which the mullahs uphold). Why should Muslims be governed instead by fallible human judgment? A state ruled by Islamic law must therefore leave little room for representative government; God's Will is not to be established by voting or public opinion.

V.S. Naipaul found these sentiments echoed all over the Islamic world. "In Islam," a prominent Pakistani Muslim told him, "there is no separation. It's a complete way of life." The noted radical Egyptian Sheikh Muhammad al-Ghazali (1917–1996) even ruled in a fatwa that Muslims who advocated the separation of religion from politics were unbelievers, and pointed out that "there is no punishment in Islam for those Muslims who kill these apostates."

The Sharia is not designed to coexist with alternative systems of governance, including one in which consensus is achieved through the ballot box. Disputed questions are matters for the *ulama*, not for voters. According to Muslim scholar Abdul Qader Abdul Aziz, the Sharia is perfect in itself, and needs no augmentation by puny human legal theorists:

> The perfection of the Shari'ah means that it is not in need for any of the previous abrogated religions [that is, Judaism and Christianity] or any human experiences—like the man made laws or any other philosophy. Therefore, any one who claims that the Muslims are in need of any such canons is considered to be a Kafer, or a disbeliever, for he belied Allah's saying: "This day I have completed your religion for you." [Holy Quran, 5:3] and His saying, . . . "Your Lord is never forgetful." [Holy Quran, 19:64]. Equal in Kufr, or disbelief, is the one who claims that the Muslims are in need for the systems of Democracy, Communism or any other ideology, without which the Muslim lived and applied the rules of Allah in matters that faced them for fourteen centuries.

To conclude our thought experiment, this means that the values at the heart of American law and society would change with a Muslim majority. In Europe, increasing Muslim populations may herald a substantial change in those societies. Sharia advocate Mohamed Elhachmi Hamdi notes that "even in the United States and Europe, there are supreme values that are embodied in the constitutions and the laws of those lands," but the Muslim world has its own set of values. Islam "has been playing this role [i.e., giver of values and laws] for the last 1,400 years, mostly for the good of Muslims, and there is no need to replace it with a set of Western values." He is, of course, arguing against replacing Islamic values with Western ones in the Islamic world; but as Muslim populations expand in Europe, the call for Islamic values will be carried westward with them.

Autocracy Even Without the Sharia

The House of Islam today is still in disarray from the period of Western colonialism, and its governments range from Sharia-based Islamic republics to more or less secular regimes based on Western models. But the rule is autocracy.

Searching for Islamic democracies, Middle East scholar Bernard Lewis uses political scientist Samuel P. Huntington's criteria for what makes a democratic state:

> [Y]ou can call a country a democracy when it has made two consecutive, peaceful changes of government via free elections. By specifying two elections, Huntington rules out regimes that follow the procedure that one acute observer has called "one man, one vote, once." So I take democracy to mean a polity where the government can be changed by elections as opposed to one where elections are changed by the government. . . .
>
> [By this criterion] predominantly Muslim regions show very few functioning democracies. Indeed, of the 53 OIC [Organization of the Islamic Conference] states, only Turkey can pass Huntington's test of democracy, and it is in many ways a troubled democracy. Among the others, one can find democratic movements and in some cases even promising democratic developments, but one cannot really say that they are democracies even to the extent that the Turkish Republic is a democracy at the present time.

Lewis continues: "Predominantly Muslim societies (Turkey, as we saw earlier, being the great exception) are ruled by a wide variety of authoritarian, autocratic, despotic, tyrannical, and totalitarian regimes." These he classifies into five major types:

• Traditional autocracies, "like Saudi Arabia and the Gulf sheikhdoms, where established dynastic regimes rest on the traditional props of usage, custom, and history." These are the states, aside from those in the fourth category below, that most explicitly base their legitimacy and law on the Qur'an and Muslim tradition. They are also . . . among the most repressive governments in the world—excepting only Marxist/Leninist dinosaurs like North Korea, Cuba and China.

• "Modernizing autocracies. These are regimes—one thinks of Jordan, Egypt, and Morocco in particular—that have their roots in traditional autocracy but are taking significant steps toward modernization and democratization. None really fits the description of liberal democracy as given above, but none is anything like a total autocracy, either." These states are caught on the fault line between the Western world and Islam, having bought into Western notions of how to constitute a society, and paying the price for it. All of these states currently suffer from increasing violence by radical Muslim groups that want to make them over into full-fledged Islamic states.

• "Fascist-style dictatorships," found today in Syria and Iraq.[4] Radical Muslims of bin Laden's ilk hold Syria's Bashar Assad (and his late father) and Iraq's Saddam Hussein in contempt for their un-Islamic ways. According to journalist Dilip Hiro, Muslim radicals have been "murderously hostile" to the Assad regime in Syria. This is chiefly because the present Syrian and Iraqi regimes are an odd hangover from the occupation of Muslim lands by European colonizers in the nineteenth and early twentieth centuries. At that time many Muslims adopted Western styles of dress and Western ways of thinking (while others reacted in the opposite fashion, by returning to the pure religion of the Qur'an and Sunnah). Saddam Hussein with his rumpled uniform and cult of personality is a sartorial and ideological stepchild of mid-twentieth-century Europe's uniformed strongmen: Hitler, Stalin, Mussolini.

• "Radical Islamic regimes. There are two of these so far, Iran and Sudan. . . . Egypt has a potent radical Islamic movement, but the Egyptian political class also has a remarkable knack for maintaining itself in power. Moreover," Lewis concludes, writing before the Taliban and Osama bin Laden had burst into the world's awareness, "the threat to the sovereign state posed by pan-Islamic radicalism has been greatly exaggerated."

• The Muslim former Soviet republics of central Asia, which Lewis characterizes as being in a period of transition. These republics are a way station from Soviet autocracy to Islamic autocracy (or perhaps secularism), and all display to varying degrees the tensions of Islamic states the world over: the tug-of-war between secularism and the Sharia.

In Azerbaijan, for example, Shi'ite Muslims from neighboring Iran have fomented discord against the secular government; in May 1996 the nation's Islamic Party leader was

4. prior to America's 2003 invasion and occupation of Iraq

arrested on espionage charges. Kyrgyzstan is another secular state. It has taken stern measures against militant Muslim groups (which it refers to collectively as "Wahhabis"), but it also shows indications of adopting the political aspects of Islam: for example, the government frowns on conversions from Islam to Christianity.

Fifty-three states, one struggling democracy. The judgment of one experienced observer of the Arab world [author David Pryce-Jones], is devastating.

Arabs have been organizing their society for half a century or so of independence, and have made a wretched job of it. A whole range of one-man rulers, whether hereditary monarchs or presidents, have proved unable or unwilling to devise political regimes that allow their people to have any say in their destinies. . . .

Perhaps Islam and representative democracy are two beautiful but incompatible ideals. Arab states have not built the institutions that are indispensable for dealing with contemporary problems. In Islam, state authority and religious authority have always gone together. Nobody so far has been able to devise some way of separating them and thus laying the foundations of a civil society.

"Islam . . . lays the ground for the values of freedom, justice and equality that are essential to democracy, more so than any other religion."

Islam Does Not Present an Obstacle to Democracy

Abdulwahab Alkebsi

The following viewpoint by Abdulwahab Alkebsi was written during the 2003 war on Iraq. American president George W. Bush justified that war in part as a way of bringing democracy to the Middle East—the region where Islam began and where it remains a vital force. Alkebsi argues that Islam values freedom, justice, and equality—principles that are essential to democracy. The fact that most Muslim nations in the Middle East and elsewhere have nondemocratic governments is not because of Islam, but in spite of it. He describes what he considers to be encouraging signs that Muslim nations are evolving toward democracy without jettisoning their Islamic values and heritage. Alkebsi is the executive director of the Center for the Study of Islam and Democracy, a Washington, D.C.–based institute.

As you read, consider the following questions:

1. What examples of democratic reforms and activism in the Arab world does Alkebsi describe?
2. Why are many people in the Middle East skeptical of U.S. efforts to promote democracy, according to the author?
3. What pragmatic question does Alkebsi ask those who maintain that Islam and democracy are not compatible?

When President George W. Bush declared [in a February 27, 2002, speech], "A new regime in Iraq would serve as a dramatic and inspiring example of freedom for other nations in the region," there was a resonance with the political-reform manifesto of Islamic moderates around the world. President Bush's vision of "a new Arab charter that champions internal reform, greater political participation, economic openness and free trade" also is consistent with Islam's clarion call for justice, equality and human dignity. A perusal of the Qur'anic evidence would leave no doubt that all these values are integral to the basic philosophy of Islam. According to the Qur'an, one of the explicit purposes of God's messengers is to offer mankind liberty, justice and equality.

True, the relationship between the state and the people in Islamic history has been one of tyranny and violence. This, however, is not because of Islam but, rather, in spite of it. Islam was, after all, in its origins a social uprising against the oppressive and discriminatory practices of Arabian society. Islam took a stand on equality of race, gender and social status at a time when equality was not the accepted norm. If anything, the tyrannical history of Muslim rulers is a reestablishment of Arabian tradition and a victory of sorts for Arab tribalism over Islamic values.

In fact there is little need to lay the theoretical groundwork for Islam's compatibility with democracy and universal values. The road map is clear and, to his credit, President Bush and his foreign-policy team are aware of it. Richard Haass, the director of the State Department's policy-planning staff, demonstrated this awareness when he remarked to the Council on Foreign Relations on Dec. 4, 2002, "Dynamic reform experiments under way in many parts of the Muslim world demonstrate that democracy and Islam are compatible."

The difficulty will be in applying the road map on the ground. But despite the loud voices of the detractors, history tells us that this is possible. Christianity, which was the pretext for the oppression and tyranny of the church and the state in medieval Europe, is the beacon of ethics and equality today. Recently there have been some encouraging signs in the Muslim world, and especially in the Arab world, where the "freedom gap" is more acute:

- Crown Prince Abdullah bin Abdulaziz of Saudi Arabia [in 2003] introduced an initiative for political and economic reforms that he envisions will become binding to all Arab nations. There is even talk among Saudi elites of an elected Parliament within six years.
- In September 2002, Moroccan citizens experienced the most transparent elections in the nation's history. An Islamist party won a sizable number of seats in Parliament, and the government accepted the results.
- In October 2002, Bahrain had a general election where citizens—both men and women—were allowed to cast their votes for Parliament and run for office.

These top-down efforts are commendable and encouraging. However, it will be very difficult for them to succeed without a serious, bottom-up movement to sustain and nourish the reforms. On this there also have been encouraging signs. The Center for the Study of Islam and Democracy (CSID) held workshops on "Islam and Democracy" in Morocco, Egypt and Yemen in October 2002. The CSID team was pleasantly surprised to find general consensus in the three countries, among moderate Islamists and secularists alike, on the need to work together to build an indigenous democracy that strives to fulfill universal rights and liberties, but also is respectful of Islam and Arab culture. CSID was able to build a network of democrats in the three countries and will continue the effort to expand the network to other countries in the region.

Despite differences in political views and backgrounds, all participants agreed that there is no way out of the dire situation in which Arabs find themselves except through democracy. Democracy, in turn, cannot be established without tackling the underlying prerequisites of human rights, women's rights, pluralism, diversity and tolerance, and making all these national priorities.

According to a recent CSID report, the following goals are paramount:
- the need to transcend the inherited authoritarian jurisprudence and to separate Islamic teachings from local customs and habits, and outdated views and interpretations;
- the need for reason to serve as the main arbiter when ad-

dressing and resolving complicated challenges that Islam faces today—great interest was shown in reviving the ideas of reformers from the turn of the last century, such as Al-Afghani, Al-Kawakibi and Muhammad Abdu;

- democratic discourse in society through the media and educational institutions—democracy has to evolve into a way of life for all members of society, not just at the governing level, in order for it to become the ultimate mechanism to express one's right to free choice and to resist oppression;
- justice as the paramount criterion in human relations, whether it is between the ruler and the ruled, the Muslim and the non-Muslim, or men and women;
- pluralism and tolerance accepted and practiced in the political, social and religious spheres.

American Credibility Is on the Line

Despite many encouraging signs, for President Bush's vision for the Middle East to take hold, and for the United States to be a positive influence in reducing the "freedom gap," this administration has to overcome an enormous credibility gap. The Arab world—and the Muslim world for that matter—does not believe that the United States is sincere about democratic reforms in their countries or in the region.

Most Arabs believe that the United States is using democracy as a pretext for achieving narrow, shortsighted U.S. interests and for stable, low, oil prices. They fault the United States for not speaking out on behalf of democracy when the culprits of tyranny are U.S. allies, but become vociferous advocates of democracy when the culprits are foes. Bush said, "America's interest in security and America's belief in liberty both lead in the same direction." Unless these words are translated into actions in Iraq and elsewhere, the United States will fail to effect positive change in the region and will gain more enemies because of its actions in Iraq. . . .

Democracy and Islam

In the long history of the world, democracy is a relatively new phenomenon. It is still developing and is far from perfect. Islam, a 1,400-year-old religion, does not, of course, prescribe democracy as we know it today, but it lays the ground for the values of freedom, justice and equality that are essential to democracy, more so than any other religion or dogma. Muslim and Arab countries have suffered for too long from oppression, authoritarianism and dictatorship. If the United States can help to bring democracy to the region, as tricky as this might be, it will become a true friend and an ally of the Muslim and Arab world. This is good for the United States, good for the region and good for the world. A prominent Arab journalist recently told me: "We are at the cusp of democratic reforms. One can either ride the wave or be carried away by it."

Muslims and Arabs neither will accept nor embrace democracy if they believe that it is foreign or alien to Islam. To those who continue to insist that Islam and democracy are not compatible, let me offer this pragmatic approach: Muslims see Islam not just as their religion, but also as their identity and culture. Some people want to promote democracy in the Muslim world by telling them: "We have this wonderful product for you. It's called democracy. It will solve all your problems. It will take care of your political, economic and social problems. It will cure your governance ills and give you prosperity. There's just one problem: It is not compatible with your religion. You have to choose either democracy or Islam." Take a guess which one they will choose!

"Western societies are now characterised by so much corruption in every sector of society and public life that it is the ideal time to present Islam as a comprehensive ideology."

Islam Is Superior to Western Democracy

Sajjad Khan

Sajjad Khan is a British Muslim and a former editorial board member of *Khilafah* magazine, a London-based publication that advocates replacing capitalism with an Islamic political system. In the following viewpoint, taken from a September 2003 article in *Khilafah*, Khan argues that democracy as practiced in the West is characterized by corruption. He argues that Western democratic values are inferior to the political values prescribed by Islam. Muslims in Great Britain and other nations should not adopt Western values but instead work toward the establishment of a society based on Islamic priniciples and teachings, he concludes.

As you read, consider the following questions:
1. What happens to Muslims and others who challenge the supremacy of democracy, according to Khan?
2. What shortcomings of democracy does the author describe?
3. How does Khan respond to the argument that religion should be kept separate from politics?

Sajjad Khan, "The Correct Political Activism for Muslims in the West," *Khilafah Magazine*, vol. 16, September 2003, pp. 8–10. Copyright © 2003 by *Khilafah Magazine*. Reproduced by permission.

"Democracy means simply the bludgeoning of the people by the people for the people."

—Oscar Wilde

"A democracy is nothing more than mob rule, where fifty-one percent of the people may take away the rights of the other forty-nine."

—Thomas Jefferson

Despite this honest appraisal by one of the West's most famous literary sons and one of the founding fathers of the United States of America and its third President, Muslims today are constantly being bulldozed into accepting democracy as part and parcel of a formation of a common identity within western society. The 'D' word has reached a mythical 'god like' stage where it is sacrosanct to even question it, despite the fact that as a system it is institutionally corrupt, produces terrible laws and has switched off millions from the political process. On top of this the 'D' word, as many Muslims are increasingly becoming aware, is in blatant contravention of the divine texts as sovereignty is for the Shari'ah [holy law], rather than with corporations who happen to have the biggest political donations budget. Yet despite all these many weaknesses, some Muslims amazingly enough still believe that joining the democratic process is a privilege and a sign of their Britishness. . . .

The main concern for us on the [*Khilafah*] magazine is therefore; how do we get Muslims to become more politically active, politically aware and more politically astute within the frameworks set down by the Shari'ah? This needs to happen without a generation of new secular and westernised fanatics emerging within the Muslim community who constantly apologise for Islamic law, dish out diatribe against other Muslims while at the same time sitting at the table of western values and militancy. . . .

Democracy and its propagation are continuously driven forward by western politicians, thinkers and the media in a way, which is almost 'missionary' at times. Needless to say we have reached a point when a person who dares to stand up to the 'D' word is immediately condemned in the harshest terms by the secular fundamentalists of the day. Indeed committing blasphemy today is easy, condemn western values and its colonial system and you are either labelled a terrorist, treated like one or air lifted in cattle class to Guantánamo Bay to be 'enlightened' by Uncle Sam's forces, the modern day guardians of all that is 'true and moral'.

Indeed so obsessed are the Western Governments in ramming their western political culture down the throats of everyone that new immigrants to Britain will now have to sing the national anthem (even though most British footballers don't know the actual words) and swear allegiance to key western values, before they can get to use a British passport. In their view a common culture is required which should bind everyone Muslim or Non-Muslim, and what should this common and magnificent culture be, it is that schools should transmit British identity through the teaching of British political history, English language and literature and an understanding of the Christian values on which western democracy is based. Clearly this is an unambiguous stance to demonstrate their quest to indoctrinate the masses.

So where does this leave Muslims in the West and in Britain, should we adopt western political values and fully integrate into western society as the recent right wing British think-tank Civitas recommends while remaining Muslims in the spiritual and personal arena. Or is there another way, a strategy that ensures Muslims don't compromise, but remain true to their own political values and culture while at the same time propagating an alternative view to the wider society.

Western Political Values

1. The western viewpoint in life divorces societal actions in this life from the hereafter and therefore ignores any accountability after death. Therefore western politicians judge actions they do in this life according to their own criteria usually the pursuit of material benefit, i.e. utilitarianism. Consequently pursuing Machiavellian methods if they are deemed necessary are considered valid political ruses or strategies, the end justifies the means, politics isn't for the faint hearted and it's a man's game, are all used as justifications for this type of behaviour.

However in contrast the Islamic politician is shaped by Islamic values and considers that all their actions will be judged in the after life and so he acts accordingly, the importance therefore of taqwa (piety) is not to be underestimated as it shapes the Islamic leadership and colours its rule. An absence of taqwa or even worse the belief in western values would soon bring corruption, which is exactly what we see day in day out in the western world. . . .

False Arguments About Democracy

The idea that democracy is modern and Islam backward is incorrect. In fact democracy . . . is the product of the Greek and Roman Empires, which predate Islam. The empires of Rome and Greece crumbled in the face of the superior political system of Islam. It was Islamic civilization that carried the banner of human progress and development to unprecedented levels. It was Islam that took science to heights from which Europe benefited and developed.

The second false argument is the idea that progress in Europe leapt from the Greeks and Romans to the enlightenment. This convenient jump of history misses out some 800 years of Islamic rule in Spain, which profoundly influenced human and scientific advance in Europe.

A third argument often put forward is the idea that democracy is universal, i.e. applicable in all places and cultures. The reality has been that stable democratic political systems have been confined to Western Europe. Democracy has failed to take root in South or Latin America, in Eastern Europe, in Russia and the former Soviet Union, in Africa, in the Arab world or in Asia (hence the importance of India to the West). The rise of Western Europe as a civilization has little to do with democracy, and a great deal to do with military colonialism, imperialism, and in particular the decline of Muslim power and the looting of its wealth.

Nor has democracy produced a global advance in the human condition. Outside of its own borders the West has been little more than a killer civilization, leaving the bulk of humanity in a pitiful state.

Jahangir Mohammed, "Democracy for Sale," http://tarbawi.tripod.com/tih/diamaukasi02.html.

---

2. The second reason is the analysis of whom the western politicians really serve. Though they boast that they work night and day for their citizens all the realities of their policies suggests otherwise. It is clear when we examine the rela-

tionships between the corporations and the politicians that the politicians have no other role than to do the bidding of the corporations who are the financiers of them and who in return receive tax cuts, and lucrative government contracts. The military is therefore no more than a resource used to further corporate interests both in the short term and longer term, which when deployed as it was in Iraq is dressed up in code words such as the 'national interest' or we are doing this to bring 'security to the American and British people'. Consequently is it any wonder that lies were told to justify the real reason for the war, not to liberate Iraq but to liberate the Profit and Loss accounts of western companies. These are the entities with the real power within capitalist societies and who demand long term stability in key markets to further their corporate agendas. The Bush administration's close marriage with the US Oil industry is a bare exposition of this reality.

3. The third issue is to highlight the fact that it is not simply politicians from one party that are involved, but it is across the entire spectrum. Contrary to popular belief there is no pluralism within western societies as all political parties broadly agree on the same fundamental values. The differences that exist are in the details not about values and like competing capitalist nations in international markets, they differ according to competing interests. In addition far from the media being a check on the system it is actually a check on individual government not on the capitalist system. This is clearly seen when we examine that the values of the media themselves are the same as those of the society in which they exist, apart from the fact they are owned by the very capitalists that also have the power within the society. . . .

4. The final point to make is that corruption in capitalist societies within the political arena is made easier by the fact that most people do not follow politics. The minority that do are largely ignored and are satisfied with their letters being published now and then in the broadsheet letters pages. Others are cleverly pushed by the regime into a cheap struggle in which they chase around for crumbs and lose sight of the real agenda. While the vast majority are content to be blinded by the 'dumb down' society obsessed with entertain-

ment, pop stars, fashion and sex. . . . In America the situation is even worse where most people don't even know where the countries their armed forces are attacking are on the map, let alone accounting them on detailed foreign policy.

There is no comparison to Islam where the state and the media actively promote politics where the people are told that accounting the ruler and critiquing his policies is an obligation, equal to prayer and fasting.

Why Politics Is Inseparable from Islam

There are still some who argue that religion and politics should not mix, that religion is for the individual and should therefore not be imposed into society. However dig a bit deeper and the individuals who advocate 'secularism' (the detachment of religion from life) as a political doctrine have no problem imposing their rule over everyone else irregardless of whether the person is secular or not.

What is also not fully understood by Muslims and Non-Muslims alike is that Politics can not be stripped from the Islamic belief, it is inherent within the Islamic ideology that it came to solve all problems and came to address the people's affairs. Bukhari narrated from Ibn Umar: The Prophet (saw) said; "The Imam is in charge and he is responsible for his citizens". Consequently there is no separation of the spiritual and the temporal within Islam, there is no separation of religion from politics or economics or foreign policy.

Consequently the Islamic ideology by its nature cannot co-exist alongside other ideologies such as communism or capitalism within the same society. Muslims may live in these societies but will find that their key political values will inevitably clash with the political culture of the host society e.g. Muslims belief that the source of legislation emanates exclusively from the creator completely contradicts with liberal capitalism's view that man is the source of legislation. . . .

Can a Muslim Adopt Western Political Values?

The simple answer to this is no. Muslims have a unique political culture as can be seen from the Prophet's life as a ruler in Medina and his successors who all governed as political leaders. Therefore the clear criteria for any action we as Muslims

50

do whether it is in prayer, hajj, or politics is to find the divine rule.

The lamentable position today is that Muslims for a variety of reasons (ignorance, personal benefit, fear of losing face, cowardice, dazzled by western civilisation) have adopted western political values without asking for any Islamic evidence. . . .

We are all aware that Islam provides the only plausible alternative to western capitalism. Western societies are now characterised by so much corruption in every sector of society and public life that it is the ideal time to present Islam as a comprehensive ideology. This requires all of us to contact western thinkers, intellectuals, think tanks and influentials so that the Islamic ideas in politics, economics, within the social system or judiciary are presented to them as the comprehensive solution for the many problems mankind faces today. This should be done in an intellectual manner with a firm and composed style i.e. with wisdom (hikmah) and beautiful speech (maw'izah hasanah). We should not underestimate the powerful effect the propagation of the Islamic thought will have amongst these people, who at present see nothing beyond the system they have. Muslims wherever they are should therefore not be satisfied with simply satisfying their own interests but must be ambassadors of Islam abiding in their own lives by the Shari'ah as well as carrying Islam to others around them. Indeed this is how Islam spread to places like Indonesia; Muslims went there and propagated Islam unapologetically obviously refusing to integrate within the host Indonesian society. Compare that approach to what we see today from those who demand integration for the Muslims living here.

*"Much of the West is addicted to a fairy-
tale version of Islam."*

Islam Is Waging a War Against the West

Don Feder

Don Feder is a former opinion writer and columnist for the
Boston Herald and the author of several books, including *A
Jewish Conservative Looks at Pagan America.* The following
viewpoint was written on the first anniversary of the September 11, 2001, terrorist attacks in New York and Washington.
In it Feder argues that Americans still have not fully learned
the lesson of that day—that the terrorist attacks were one
chapter in a long-standing war of Islam against the rest of the
world, particularly the United States and other Western nations. He argues that the September 11 terrorists were practicing Muslims and that Islamic religious authorities have
generally either endorsed or rationalized the attacks and
other acts of terrorism.

As you read, consider the following questions:

1. What examples of Islamic violence does Feder describe?
2. What criticisms does Feder make about the
   pronouncements of President George W. Bush and Bush
   administration officials regarding Islam?
3. What contrast does Feder draw between Islam and
   Christianity in connection to violence?

People keep asking me what we learned from September 11, 2001 and the deaths of 3,000 of our fellow citizens. I'm tempted to say: Absolutely nothing. (Who was it who remarked that the lessons of history are the last things we ever learn?)

Among the many unlearned lessons of Day-Which-Will-Live-In-Infamy-II—the necessity to control our borders, the need for a patriotic renewal and the importance of combatting multiculturalism—the most significant is the nature of Islam. You will note that I do not say militant Islam, or radical Islam, or Islamic extremism or other such weasel words—but Islam, period.

Every one of the hijackers who flew airliners into the World Trade Center and Pentagon were professing and practicing Moslems, as is [terrorist leader] Osama bin Laden. The Al Qaeda network [responsible for the attacks] is based in Moslem countries and supported financially by pious Moslems in Saudi Arabia.

The overwhelming majority of Moslem religious authorities who've spoken out on the subject, including those at the main mosque in Mecca and Egypt's prestigious Al Azar University, either endorse or rationalize acts of terrorism. On a day when Americans were incinerated or buried under tons of rubble, from Nigeria to Indonesia, Moslems celebrated in the streets.

Sept. 11 was one chapter in a 1,400-year jihad. Every day, the World Trade Center massacre is reenacted on a smaller scale somewhere in the Third World—Jewish women and children are burned alive in a bus on the West Bank, a missionary is beheaded in the Philippines, gunmen shoot up a church in Pakistan (deliberately firing into the prostrate bodies of women trying to shield their children), ancient monasteries and convents are destroyed in Kosovo, a woman is sentenced to death for adultery in Nigeria, Hindus are murdered in the Kashmir, a nun is found beheaded in Baghdad—and the beat goes on.

Genocide in the Sudan, ethnic cleansing in the Balkans, religious persecution in Saudi Arabia, calls for another holocaust in mosques from Mecca to Gaza, the imposition of Islamic law in Nigeria, forced conversions in Indonesia, syna-

gogues burned in France, Jews attacked across Europe—
these are everyday events, as Third World and much of the
First slowly turns Islamic green.

And still our leaders, from President [George W.] Bush
on down, insist on peddling the absurdity that Islam is a religion of peace—a creed of kindness and benevolence tragi-
cally and inexplicably corrupted by fanatics.

At a conference, I recently had an exchange with Tom
Ridge, the Director of Homeland Security, wherein I questioned the governor on Islam a la Hans Christian Andersen.
Ridge replied that Islam was indeed a pacific faith corrupted
by a handful of heretics. I replied that the "handful" is in the
hundreds of millions and—as far as I can see—it's the
Moslems who aren't trying to kill us who've misinterpreted
their religion.

Why this reluctance to confront manifest reality? The
reason lies partly with our absurd foreign policy. We've declared certain Moslem nations to be our loyal allies—including Saudi Arabia, Egypt and Jordan. We wouldn't want to
offend these dear friends by saying something unflattering
about their bloody, butcherly, dark ages faith.

Then too, Americans are naturally benevolent. Most of us
are taught from childhood that religion is good (and it
doesn't matter which religion). As long as little Johnny believes in God and goodness, it's inconsequential whether he
lights candles, wears a skull cap to services or prays in the direction of Mecca.

This works with every religion except Islam.

Consider the following: Of the three major monotheistic
religions, one was started by a lawgiver, one by a man of
peace (try to imagine Mohammed telling his followers to
turn the other cheek) and one by a warrior. Mohammed led
men into battle. The essence of his message is holy
war—slaughtering your enemies for the glory of Allah. He
even advised his followers to negotiate phony truces to lull
their enemies.

For almost 1,400 years, that has been the reality of Islam.
Within a century after the death of Mohammed, Islam
spread throughout the Middle East and across North Africa.
It overran the Iberian peninsula and was finally stopped in

southern France. It spread eastward as far as the southern Philippines. It was not propagated by fresh-faced young men knocking on doors and announcing: "Hello. I'm from your local mosque. Have you considered the Koran?" It was spread by force—conversion by the sword. To a large extent, it still is.

Islamists Target America

America has become a focus of Islamist rage because, when the terrorists seek to wreak their havoc around the world, whether in Israel, Pakistan, Malaysia, Indonesia, or Afghanistan, we stand in their way, thwart their intentions, and defeat their fighters. We also undercut their beliefs by urging the equality of women and individual and religious freedom. They are rendered impotent in all but death as long as American military might and American cultural power stands in their way.

Now, as Islamist terrorists repeat endlessly, their strategic goal must now be to make the United States retreat so that they can achieve Islamist rule elsewhere.

Paul Marshall, *National Review Online*, November 26, 2002.

Some will respond that all religions go through periods of violence, usually in their infancy. Christianity had its crusades and Inquisition, its forced conversions and expulsions. But the evil committed in the name of Christ happened centuries ago. The evil committed in the name of the Prophet is going on now, as you read these words. Of 22 conflicts in the Third World, 20 involve Moslems versus someone else. Coincidence? In his brilliant book, "Clash of Cultures and the Remaking of World Order," Samuel Huntington speaks of Islam's "bloody borders."

There is no Methodist Jihad, no Hasidic holy warriors, no Southern Baptist suicide bombers, no Mormon elders preaching the annihilation of members of other faiths.

Islam is a warrior religion—the perfect vessel for fanatics, the violence-prone, the envious and haters of all stripes. This is one reason why Islam is making so many converts among the peaceable denizens of our prison system.

Still, much of the West is addicted to a fairy-tale version of Islam. Christian and Jewish clergy fall all over themselves to have interfaith services with imams. Representatives of Moslem groups are invited to the White House. The president signs a Ramadan declaration. In California, public schools ask children to role-play at being Moslems. Our universities take carefully selected verses from the Koran and present them as the essence of the faith. All that's needed is a Moslem character on "Sesame Street." Look—it's the Jihad Monster!

This perspective engenders a fatally false sense of security. Imagine, in 1940, [British prime minister] Winston Churchill taking to the airwaves to announce that Nazism was an ideology of peace which, regrettably, had been perverted by a few fanatics like Hitler and Goebbels. But most storm troopers and SS men are fine fellows—your friends and neighbors.

For the first thousand years of its history—from the death of Mohammed to the 17th. century decline of the Ottoman empire, Islam was an expansionist force. For the next 300 years, as the West rose to preeminence, Islam receded. For the past four decades—fueled by Arab oil wealth, a surplus population in the Middle East, the waning of the West and the rise of more virulent strains of the faith (Shiism, Wahhabism, Sunni fundamentalism)—Islam is expanding once more. Round and round she goes and where she stops nobody knows.

Due to Moslem immigration and aggressive proselytizing among the underclass, Islam is being exported to the West. Moslem populations are burgeoning throughout Western Europe. (In southern France, there are said to be more mosques than churches.) In Judeo-Christian America, Islam is the fastest growing religion. It's also spreading down the coast of West Africa, through the Balkans (after Serbia, Macedonia is the next target) and up from Mindanao in the Philippines.

Wherever it comes, Islam brings its delightful customs— child marriages, female circumcisions, rabid anti-Semitism, terrorism and support for terrorism and a virulent intolerance of other faiths.

Am I suggesting we declare war on 900 million Moslems? The question is irrelevant—many of them have declared war on us. When one side knows it's at war and the other thinks peace and brotherhood prevail, guess who wins?

"Economics, more specifically greed, is the primary reason for the clash between Islam and the West."

America Is Waging a War Against Islam

Enver Masud

Enver Masud, an engineering management consultant who became a public speaker and newspaper columnist, is the author of *The War on Islam*, from which the following viewpoint is excerpted. He argues that Islam respects other faiths, especially Judaism and Christianity, and is not trying to take over the world. Rather, the clash between Islamic and Western countries is caused by the desire of the United States to dominate the world and control global resources and markets. Masud also contends that the United States uses its support of the Jewish state of Israel to divide and control the Muslim world. American foreign policy, not Islam, is to blame for whatever "clash" may exist between Islam and the West, he concludes.

As you read, consider the following questions:

1. What three words sum up the clash between Islam and the West, according to Masud?
2. What examples of peace and cooperation between Muslims, Christians, and Jews does the author describe?
3. What, according to Masud, has been the primary goal of U.S. foreign policy since World War II?

Enver Masud, *The War on Islam*. Arlington, VA: Madrasah Books, 2003.
Copyright © 2003 by Enver Masud. Reproduced by permission.

The clash between Islam and the West, is not a clash between Islam and Christianity worthy of war. The clash between Islam and the West is not a clash between Islam and Judaism worthy of war. The clash between Islam and the West is not a clash of civilizations worthy of war.

The clash between Islam and the West may be summed up in three words: justice versus greed.

Muslims, Christians, Jews

The *Quran*—the Word of God for Muslims—states:

> O mankind! We created you from a single soul, male and female, and made you into nations and tribes, so that you may come to know one another. Truly, the most honored of you in God's sight is the greatest of you in piety.

Thus, Islam, perhaps like no other religion, declares to Muslims the sanctity of all "nations and tribes." What may surprise Christians and Jews, and even many Muslims, is that the *Quran* refers to them all as "muslim."

Muhammad Asad, born Leopold Weiss in Poland in 1900, in his interpretation of the *Quran* wrote:

> When his contemporaries heard the words islam and muslim, they understood them as denoting man's "self-surrender to God" and "one who surrenders himself to God," without limiting himself to any specific community or denomination—e.g., in 3:67, where Abraham is spoken of as having "surrendered himself unto God" (kana musliman), or in 3:52 where the disciples of Jesus say, "Bear thou witness that we have surrendered ourselves unto God (bianna musliman)." In Arabic, this original meaning has remained unimpaired, and no Arab scholar has ever become oblivious of the wide connotation of these terms.

The three faiths share the Abrahamic heritage, the same values, and revere many of the same prophets. The prophets of Judaism and Christianity, are also Islam's prophets.

Muslims, Christians, Jews once lived in peace in Palestine—all three referred to God as Allah. The three faiths thrived in Muslim Spain until its fall to Christian armies. [The philosopher] Maimonides, highly revered among Jews, studied and practiced in Muslim Spain.

With the fall of Muslim Spain to Christian armies in 1492, Muslims and Jews were expelled or forced to convert to Christianity. The Jews who chose to convert and remain in Spain, were called maranos (pigs) by the Christians. Islam teaches that "the most excellent jihad is for the conquest of self." It teaches Muslims to speak out against oppression, and to fight if necessary for justice. This is jihad. Mainly Muslim Turkey has been a member of NATO since 1952. Virtually every Muslim country supported the U.S. "war on terror" until it degenerated into an excuse for a crackdown on Muslims by governments across the world. While leading Christian evangelists, and the hawks in U.S. government, push for war on Iraq, predominantly Christian Europe is opposed to war.[1] According to the *Guardian*, "Church leaders including the new Archbishop of Canterbury, Rowan Williams, have questioned the legality and morality of an American-led assault on Iraq in a strongly worded declaration handed to Downing Street." Non-Muslim organizations in the U.S. have been demonstrating in opposition to the war.

Many Jews support statehood for the Christians and Muslims in Palestine. "Britain's chief rabbi, Jonathon Sacks, head of the Jewish community in the U.K. and the Commonwealth for 11 years, warns that Israel's stance towards Palestinians is incompatible with Judaism," according to *BBC News*. Naturei Karta International, an Orthodox Jewish organization, has printed on its stationery: "Pray for the peaceful dismantling of the Zionist State."

Economic Causes

But, there have been, and perhaps there always will be, clashes both among and between peoples and nations, and within civilizations.

The clash between the Dalits—the lowest caste in India, and the upper castes, is a clash that has persisted for centuries. Europe, throughout its history, has been ravaged by clashes within Christianity. Muslims have fought wars with Muslims.

For the most part, the underlying reason for these clashes is economic. Economics, more specifically greed, is the pri-

---

1. After months of debate and demonstrations, America led an invasion of Iraq in March 2003 that deposed Iraq's leader, Saddam Hussein.

mary reason for the clash between Islam and the West.

The U.S. desire to control the world's resources and markets, its abject surrender to the zionists regardless of the cost to Americans and others, and the virtual exclusion of dissenting voices from the national dialogue, is very likely to lead to war.

What's evident from world history is that the U.S. will be going to a war which will benefit a few, at the expense of many. The clash over the control of resources and markets is not new.

Control of the World's Resources and Markets

Following the fall of Muslim Spain in 1492, Europeans spread out over the world—to the Americas, Africa, Asia, Australia. Millions of natives in those continents were brutalized, enslaved, killed.

By some accounts, 15 million natives of North America perished, 50 million natives of South America perished, and 100 to 200 million Africans perished—"since ten people had to be killed for one to be taken alive during capture by the slave-dealers."

By the end of the 18th century, the Spanish, Portuguese, Dutch, British, and French ruled much of the world.

In the mid-twentieth century, when the British Empire was crumbling, and the colonial powers were pulling out from Asia and Africa, they drew up national boundaries for their continuing benefit, and the U.S. Empire began to take shape.

The U.S. had fought for control of the world's resources and markets while keeping the true reasons for war from Americans.

Major General Smedley D. Butler, recipient of two Congressional Medals of Honor, described his experience in the U.S. Marine Corps:

> War is just a racket. . . I helped make Mexico, especially Tampico, safe for American oil interests in 1914. I helped make Haiti and Cuba a decent place for the National City Bank boys to collect revenues in. I helped in the raping of half a dozen Central American republics for the benefits of Wall Street. The record of racketeering is long. I helped purify Nicaragua for the international banking house of Brown

Brothers in 1909. . . I brought light to the Dominican Republic for American sugar interests in 1916. In China I helped to see to it that Standard Oil went its way unmolested.

The primary goal of U.S. foreign policy, defined after World War II, assured a continuing clash between the U.S., and weaker, resource-rich nations.

George Kennan, recipient of the Albert Einstein Peace Prize, chairman of the Policy Planning Staff at the State Department, wrote in the top secret Policy Planning Study No. 23:

We have about 50% of the world's wealth, but only 6.3% of its population. . . . Our real task in the coming period is to devise a pattern of relationships which will permit us to maintain this position of disparity.

While U.S. policy advisors may differ on the specific timing and means, this militant foreign policy—often backed up by assassination of opponents (aka "regime change"), military coups, terrorism—has powerful proponents.

Former National Security Advisor to President Carter, Zbigniew Brzezinski, writes in The Grand Chessboard (1997):

A power that dominates Eurasia [the territory east of Germany and Poland, stretching all the way through Russia and China to the Pacific Ocean—including the Middle East and most of the Indian subcontinent] would control two of the world's three most advanced and economically productive regions. A mere glance at the map also suggests that control over Eurasia would almost automatically entail Africa's subordination, rendering the Western Hemisphere and Oceania geopolitically peripheral to the world's central continent. About 75 per cent of the world's people live in Eurasia, and most of the world's physical wealth is there as well, both in its enterprises and underneath its soil. Eurasia accounts for 60 per cent of the world's GNP and about three-fourths of the world's known energy resources.

The key to controlling Eurasia, says Brzezinski, is controlling the Central Asian Republics. "The three grand imperatives of imperial geostrategy are to prevent collusion and maintain security dependence among the vassals, to keep tributaries pliant and protected, and to keep the barbarians from coming together," he adds.

According to the *Los Angeles Times*:

Behind a veil of secret agreements, the United States is creating a ring of new and expanded military bases that encircle Afghanistan and enhance the armed forces' ability to strike targets throughout much of the Muslim world.

Since Sept. 11 [2001], according to Pentagon sources, military tent cities have sprung up at 13 locations in nine countries neighboring Afghanistan, . . . they may also increase prospects for renewed terrorist attacks on Americans. . . . On any given day before Sept. 11, according to the Defense Department, more than 60,000 military personnel were conducting temporary operations and exercises in about 100 countries.

Uncritical Support of the Apartheid State of Israel

The unresolved issue of Israel helps keep the "barbarians"—presumably, the Muslim nations of the Middle East, Africa, and Central Asia—from coming together. The U.S.—which displayed exceptional zeal in implementing UN Security Council resolutions against Iraq—has displayed the same zeal in blocking implementation of UN Security Council resolutions against Israel.

Leahy. © by Cartoonists & Writers Syndicate. Reproduced by permission.

UN Security Council Resolution 242 of 1967 which emphasizes "the inadmissibility of the acquisition of territory by war," and requires the "withdrawal of Israeli armed forces from territories[2] occupied in the recent conflict," has yet to be implemented. Meanwhile the U.S. sends billions of dollars in aid to Israel.

While the U.S. pushes for war on Iraq, and maintains no-fly zones in Northern and Southern Iraq, under the U.S. interpretation of UN Security Council Resolution 687 (with which most others disagree), the U.S. ignores Article 14 of the same resolution which has "the goal of establishing in the Middle East a zone free from weapons of mass destruction and all missiles for their delivery and the objective of a global ban on chemical weapons" for all the nations in the region—including Israel which is known to possess chemical and biological weapons, and 200 to 400 nuclear weapons and the missiles to deliver them.

The United States, which claims to promote democracy around the world, continues its uncritical support of the apartheid state of Israel (read *Israel: An Apartheid State* by Israeli lawyer, Dr. Uri Davis), and its unlawful occupation of Palestine. Fortunately, for now the "barbarians" and most of the "civilized" world appear to be standing on the side of justice in the Middle East.

Need to Justify U.S. Military Spending

New military bases, such as those established in Central Asia during the Afghan war, support the defense establishment's need to justify military spending.

According to Lawrence J. Korb, assistant secretary in the Defense Department during the Reagan administration:

> In 1985, at the height of the Reagan build-up, the United States and the Soviet Union spent equal amounts on defense; now Russia spends only one-sixth of what the United States spends. . . . Our NATO allies spend three times more on defense than Russia. Israel spends as much as Iraq and Iran combined. South Korea spends nine times more on defense than North Korea. And Japan spends more on defense than China.

The U.S. covert operations budget alone is more than double the total defense budget of the "rogue states"—Cuba, Iran, Iraq, Libya, North Korea, Syria.

2. These include Gaza and the West Bank.

"For 45 years of the Cold War we were in an arms race with the Soviet Union. Now it appears we're in an arms race with ourselves," says Admiral Eugene Carroll, Jr., U.S. Navy (Ret.), Deputy Director, Center for Defense Information.

Former Defense Secretary [Robert] McNamara, in his 1989 testimony before the Senate Budget Committee, said U.S. defense spending could safely be cut in half.

The Real Rogue and International Outlaw

Multi-billionaire George Soros, writes in *Open Society: Reforming Global Capitalism:* "The United States has become the greatest obstacle to establishing the rule of law in international affairs."

According to a survey done for the Chicago Council on Foreign Relations and the German Marshall Fund of the U.S., "a majority of people in six European countries believe American foreign policy is partly to blame for the Sept. 11 attacks."

The U.S. stands virtually alone against the world in efforts to build a safer, better world. For example:

International Covenant on Economic, Social, and Cultural Rights (1966) was unanimously approved by the UN General Assembly but not ratified by the U.S.

Anti-Ballistic Missile Treaty (1972) was signed and ratified by the U.S. and USSR, but overturned by President [George W.] Bush.

Convention on the Elimination of Discrimination Against Women (1979) was ratified by more than 150 governments but not the U.S.

UN Convention on the Law of the Sea (1982) was supported by 130 governments but never ratified by the U.S.

Convention on the Rights of the Child (1989) was ratified by 187 governments but not the U.S.

Comprehensive Test Ban Treaty (1996) was signed by President Clinton, ratified by all NATO allies and Russia, voted down by the U.S. Senate, and is opposed by President [George W.] Bush.

Kyoto Protocol (1997) sets targets for emissions which cause global warming awaits ratification by the U.S.

Chemical Weapons Convention (1998) was crippled by the

U.S. by limiting what may be inspected in the U.S.

Biological Weapons Convention (2001) was signed by 144 countries, but the U.S. rejected the "verification protocol."

Nonproliferation and Test Ban Treaties (2002) have been jeopardized by the U.S. by its announcement to build and use small, tactical, nuclear weapons.

International Criminal Court (July 1, 2002) was backed by 74 countries, signed by President Clinton, but was fiercely opposed by the U.S. unless American citizens were given immunity from war crimes prosecutions.

The opposition by a signatory to the treaty undermines the entire system of international law.

The Need for Dialogue

Civilized nations—nations that respect the rule of law—solve economic clashes with dialogue, not war.

But the voracious U.S. appetite for resources and markets, the desire to control those resources and markets, the uncritical U.S. support of Israel, and the need to justify military spending, are driving the U.S. to war. This is bound to create more resentment, and perhaps retaliation.

Those who stand to benefit by war, have characterized opposition to U.S. domination as a "clash of civilizations." They are not interested in just agreements freely negotiated. They understand only the language of realpolitik—a euphemism for state-sponsored terrorism.

Fortunately, due to an increasingly multi-cultural society, and the Internet, the world is waking up. Many see the clash between Islam and the West for what it is: a clash of justice versus greed.

The September 11, 2001 attack on America may have been prevented, had there been an honest exchange of dissenting views presented to Americans. President John F. Kennedy said: "Those who make peaceful revolution impossible will make violent revolution inevitable." Only through dialogue is "peaceful revolution" possible.

Periodical Bibliography

The following articles have been selected to supplement the diverse views presented in this chapter.

Abdelwahab El-Affendi — "Do Muslims Deserve Democracy? What's Stopping Democracy from Taking Root in Muslim Countries?" *New Internationalist*, May 2002.

Scott Alexander — "Don't Know Much About Islam? The Editors Interview Scott Alexander," *U.S. Catholic*, August 2003.

Mahmood Butt — "Conflict Unending?" *World & I*, July 2003.

Eliot A. Cohen — "World War IV," *Wall Street Journal*, November 20, 2001.

Michael J. Fischer — "Islam: The Odd Civilization Out?" *New Perspectives Quarterly*, Winter 2002.

Anthony Flew — "Islam's War Against the West," *Free Inquiry*, Spring 2002.

Nader Hashemi — "Islam, Democracy, and Alexis de Tocqueville," *Queen's Quarterly*, Spring 2003.

Pervez Hoodbhoy — "Muslims and the West After September 11," *Free Inquiry*, Spring 2002.

Ronald Inglehart and Pippa Norris — "The True Clash of Civilizations," *Foreign Policy*, March/April 2003

Muqtedar Khan — "Prospects for Muslim Democracy: The Role of U.S. Policy," *Middle East Policy*, Fall 2003.

Glenn E. Perry — "Huntington and His Critics: The West and Islam," *Arab Studies Quarterly*, Winter 2002.

Edward W. Said — "The Clash of Ignorance," *Nation*, October 22, 2001.

Jonathan Schanzer — "At War with Whom?" *Doublethink*, Spring 2002.

Douglas Streusand — "Clash of Civilizations?" *World & I*, July 2003.

Lisa Wedeen — "Beyond the Crusades: Why Huntington, and Bin Laden, Are Wrong," *Middle East Policy*, Summer 2003.

CHAPTER 2

Does Islam Promote Terrorism and Violence?

Chapter Preface

In 1998 Osama bin Laden and his associates issued a fatwa—a judicial opinion interpreting Islamic religious and legal teachings. They asserted in the fatwa that it was the religious duty of Muslims to kill Americans in order to liberate Islam's holy sites in Saudi Arabia. They also demanded that American military forces withdraw from all the "lands of Islam." These prescriptions were justified using several passages from the Koran including the command to "fight the pagans all together as they fight you all together." Bin Laden's fatwa was acted on with deadly results on September 11, 2001, when members of his organization al-Qaeda carried out terrorist attacks that killed nearly three thousand people in New York City and Washington, D.C. These actions, and bin Laden's words, are for some observers proof that Islam promotes terrorism and violence in the guise of "holy war" against infidels.

However, many Muslims in America and elsewhere were quick to condemn the September 11 attacks and reject the fatwa used to justify them. They argued that Islam is not a violent religion and that extremists such as bin Laden distort its teachings. On October 17, 2001, for instance, the Canadian office of the Council on American-Islamic Relations (CAIR) and the Canadian Muslim Civil Liberties Association issued a joint statement claiming that "Islam respects the sacredness of life, and rejects any express statement or tacit insinuation that Muslims should harm innocent people." They also stated that teachings that ran counter to this were "contrary to the letter and spirit of Islam." They and other scholars and organizations argue that while Islamic teachings may justify war for self-defense or to fight oppression, such war must be waged in a way that preserves the lives of innocents and avoids harm to the environment. They have also questioned bin Laden's standing to issue a fatwa, noting that he is neither a head of a sovereign government nor a trained religious jurist.

Not everyone agrees that bin Laden's views represent a fringe element within Islam. Scholar Robert Spencer asserts, for example, that bin Laden's fatwa "is firmly rooted in Islamic law" and that Islam's classical texts and teachings are more closely aligned with bin Laden's views than those of his critics. Since the September 11 attacks, Muslims and non-Muslims alike have been arguing vociferously about the true nature of Islam. The following selections examine whether bin Laden's views are truly representative of Islam and whether that religion can be said to promote violence and terrorism.

"It seems plain that Islam is confronted by the problem of religious violence in ways that other religions are not."

Islam Promotes Terrorism and Violence

Richard D. Connerney

The following viewpoint by Richard D. Connerney was written shortly after the September 11, 2001, terrorist attacks on America. The attacks, which killed approximately three thousand people, were carried out by members of al-Qaeda, an Islamic terrorist organization. Connerney, then a visiting professor of religion at Iona College in New York, witnessed the destruction of the World Trade Center towers—an event that he says caused him to rethink Islam and its concept of jihad. He notes that Islam's sacred writings can be interpreted to justify violence against nonbelievers, and that Islam for much of its history has been associated with such violence—including terrorism—more than have other religions. He attributes Islam's propensity for violence to the fact that Islam originated in conjunction with a military empire and thus has never developed the traditions of existing outside a theocratic Islamic state. Connerney is the author of *Safe in Heaven Dead* and former editor of *Tricycle: The Buddhist Review*.

As you read, consider the following questions:

1. What did Connerney teach his students about Islam prior to September 11?
2. Why is the Koran a difficult text to interpret, according to the author?
3. What main distinction does Connerney make between Islam and other religions?

Richard D. Connerney, "Islam: Religion of the Sword?" www.salon.com, October 11, 2001. Copyright © 2001 by *Salon*, www.salonmagazine.com. Reproduced by permission.

O n Sept. 9 [2001], I was giving an introductory lecture to my Religion 203 weekend seminar at Iona College. I began as usual with some definitions of some commonly heard terms used in the study of religion. As an example on the term "fundamentalism," I wrote the word "jihad" on the board. I explained that the word could be interpreted as "religious war," but that it was perhaps more accurately translated as "struggle," meaning simply that Muslims were encouraged to struggle for their religion.

"Only an Islamic fundamentalist would interpret it as a rationalization for physical violence," I continued. "The vast majority of Muslims define jihad as the jihad al'akbar, or the greater warfare, meaning to wage war against human ignorance and cruelty."

The entire class wrote what I had said down in their notebooks. Nobody asked any questions.

September 11

Two days later, I witnessed the destruction of the World Trade Center towers. I was unlucky enough to see it happen from the rooftop of my apartment in Brooklyn. It was my day off from teaching and I had just got out of bed. My Russian neighbor knocked on my door to tell me that there had been an accident in Manhattan and that I should take a look from my roof. So I invited her in and we climbed through the roof from where I had a picture-perfect view of the south tip of Manhattan. It did not seem that bad when I first saw it. An accident, I assumed—bad, yes, catastrophic, no.

"Was the pilot drunk?" my neighbor, Olga, laughed.

I laughed too. "He must have been," I agreed.

"Look," I said, "here comes another one."

"He must be drunk too."

It looked green to me—although I am told now that it was blue, a blue United 767. The morning light played tricks on me and it looked a dark shade of green. It flew over Staten Island and New York Harbor. It looked like it was going to fly up the Hudson River.

I do not need to say anymore about what happened next. We have all seen the pictures. The smoke, the chaos and the unimaginable cruelty of the events are the closest I have ever

71

come or want to come to having an apocalyptic vision. I did not believe it had happened, even when I saw the fireball bulging out from the tower. The pandemonium approached the surreal when charred office memos from the towers floated over the East River and landed on my roof. It was letterhead from a company called Marsh, 1 World Trade Center, 98th floor. I looked at it in tears and considered that it might have been in the hands of a secretary in the towers just moments before. . . .

Several weeks later, when I met my class again, there were many questions about jihad. And not only among my students but also in my own mind. Since the attacks, great care has been taken to emphasize that Osama bin Laden and the al-Qaida terrorist network do not represent Islam or the concept of jihad as presented in the Quran. Everybody certainly wishes that this were true, that Islam is a religion of peace, as the president said, and that the bin Ladens of the world are nothing more than aberrations in the history of religion.

This is the viewpoint of James Reston, author of "Warriors of God: Richard the Lionheart and Saladin in the Third Crusade." During a recent interview on NPR, Reston likened bin Laden and his terrorists to the cult of the Assassins, a medieval group of Islamic heretics who used assassination to intimidate adversaries. "Bin Laden no more represents Islam than [Jim] Jones and David Koresh represent Christianity," he said.

Other scholars and writers, both Western and Islamic, have endorsed the same position repeatedly in the press over the last months. They are challenged by the messages of the terrorists themselves who cite the Quran with as much familiarity as any academic does and who have a vastly different interpretation.

Interpreting the Quran

Yet, when asked about the origin of jihad as expressed in the Quran, Reston and the others get a bit tongue-tied. There are several reasons for this. The Quran is a notoriously difficult text to understand in some ways. For one thing, it lacks almost any sense of context: Verses are addressed to mysterious Yous and Theys from an equally mysterious We. Moreover, the subject of the verses follow no discernible pattern, moving from questions of jurisprudence to theological and mythological concerns and back again, sometimes without any apparent pattern. For this reason, the Quran has inspired an extensive body of exegetical texts that purport to explain the original meaning of the text. Nevertheless, untangling the original meaning, or creating a distinct context in which to interpret the verses, is a nightmarish problem.

Islam and Violence

For all too many, being a serious Muslim means doing Allah's work by any means necessary. Of course, most Muslims will never be terrorists. The problem is that for all its schisms, sects and multiplicity of voices, Islam's violent elements are rooted in its central texts. It is unlikely that the voices of moderation will ultimately silence the militants, because the militants will always be able to make the case that they are standing for the true expression of the faith. Liberal Muslims have not established a viable alternative interpretation of the relevant verses in the Qur'an. "When liberal Muslims declare that Sept. 11 was an atrocity contrary to the Koran," observes Farrukh Dhondy, "the majority of Muslims around the world don't believe them. They accept the interpretation of fundamentalists, whom liberal Muslims have allowed to remain unchallenged.". . .

Violent Islam has the enemy (us) and the scriptural justification (in the Qur'an) to keep pushing until they win—that is, until the West is Islamicized. And moderate Islam is essentially powerless to stop it.

Robert Spencer, *Islam Unveiled*, 2002.

Thus the question of what the Quran has to say about jihad, or any other subject, is exceedingly difficult. As could be expected from a document that arises in an environment of unceasing internecine warfare, as the Arabian Peninsula was in the seventh century, the Quran contains no argument for pacifism. To the contrary, it makes conflict a requirement of the new faith. "Fighting is obligatory for you, much as you dislike it" (2:216). Those who remain at home during wartime are repeatedly denigrated as shirkers (e.g., 9:37) and warned that hellfire is hotter than the heat of battle (e.g., 9:81).

At times, the Quran does prohibit aggression (2:189): "God

does not love aggressors." At other times, however, the text is ambiguous on this point, as in 9:121: "Believers, make war on the infidels who dwell around you, be firm with them." Perhaps the best way to sum up the hawkish attitude of the Quran is to note that the index to the Penguin edition of the Quran contains over 40 entries for "war," and no entries for "peace."

Some religious texts, including parts of both the Bible and the Quran, are the hermeneutic equivalent of a Rorschach test—their original meaning is so obscure that any interpretation reveals more about the reader than it does about the author. In the same way that the Book of Revelations has been cited as a warning about any world ruler from Napoleon to Ronald Wilson Reagan (count the letters in his name—666), the Quran can be used to support an almost endless variety of viewpoints and practices.

In this case, we may be tempted to go back to the interpretation of the early Muslim community. They lived closer to the text's original composition, so perhaps they knew what it really meant. I certainly hope not.

The unfortunate truth of the matter is that Muslim violence against the civilian populations of other religions goes right back to the origin of Islam in the seventh century A.D. According to Islamic holy texts, Muhammad himself presided over the extermination of the Jews of Khaybar in 629, an event that the Quran calls a "glorious victory" (48:1). (To be fair some historians have questioned the historicity of this massacre.) In addition, despite the later evenhandedness of rulers like Saladin, the original Islamic conquest of Jerusalem was a bloody affair, as was the introduction of Islam to North Africa and India.

Thus, jihad is historically and textually ambivalent. It could be interpreted as a simple struggle with oneself, like wrestling with your conscience. It could also, however, be interpreted as acts of physical violence against non-Muslims. There might be rules regarding civilian noncombatants—and then again, there might not be. The idea of jihad, like many ideas in the Quran, is a Janus-faced idea with two or more possible interpretations, all supported by scripture. Historically, numerous interpretations have been drawn from the Quran in relation to jihad by different groups with different agendas. A Rorschach test.

To an extent, this ambivalence exists in many religions, including Judaism and Christianity. Muslims are not the only ones to have waged wars in the name of religion. So have Christians, Jews, Hindus and Buddhists. The validity of the comparison ends there, however. It seems plain that Islam is confronted by the problem of religious violence in ways that other religions are not. In the world today, the locus of most religious violence is the Muslim world. And Islam is the only religion that has spawned a wandering group of holy warriors, traveling from conflict to conflict fighting the enemies of Islam wherever they see them—in Bosnia, Chechnya, Afghanistan.

Fundamentalism

There are some who say that the real antagonists are fundamentalism and modernity, that the real conflict is between a medieval mind-set and a modern one. In a recent *New York Times Magazine* article, Andrew Sullivan stated, "This surely is a religious war—but not of Islam versus Christianity and Judaism. Rather, it is a war of fundamentalism against faiths of all kinds that are at peace with freedom and modernity."

There is some truth to this, but it does not fully explain the situation. Fundamentalism, as a literal and nonhistoric approach to religious scripture, exists in every tradition, but only in Islam does it go hand in hand with widespread violence. Yes, Southern preachers occasionally get carried away, and yes, Hindu fundamentalists cause intermittent communal violence in the Deccan subcontinent. Neither of these two fundamentalisms, however, has produced the same types of problems as Islam. It is not Hindu fundamentalists or Southern Baptists that generally become international terrorists.

What Is Different About Islam?

What is the difference then between Islam and other world faiths? Is there something inherent in the history and texts of the religion that lead to this behavior?

I think that there is.

At the core of Islamic history is the fact of the unification of the tribes of Arabia into a powerful medieval military force, one that overran the waning power of the Byzantine Empire and the Persians in the Levant. Islam, from its inception, is a political as well as a religious movement, and the themes of religion, politics and law are inseparable in the Quran and in Islam as a whole. In short, Islam does not have a religious history apart from its political history.

This is in distinction from Judaism and Christianity, in which the religious community both predates and postdates the existence of a Jewish or Christian political state. Judaism already exists as a faith in the quasihistorical Age of the Patriarchs (circa 2000–1300 B.C.) before the establishment of the Kingdom of Israel, and Judaism continues to exist and develop as a religious community after the Babylonian Captivity, the Roman occupation, the fall of Jerusalem in 70 A.D. and throughout the Diaspora up to the year 1948.

In a similar way Christianity, self-consciously apolitical in its origin, exists for centuries in a Roman/pagan context until the conversion of Emperor Constantine in 325 A.D.

This development of the religious community outside of the halls of political power gives both Judaism and Christianity the flexibility to adapt to the secular concept of the separation of church and state that comes out of the Enlightenment, and to embrace ideas of modernity and secular civil society. Put simply, neither faith requires the existence of a theocratic state to function fully as a religion because both their origins and endpoints exist above and beyond concerns of statehood.

Not so with Islam. The fact of Muslim military might is the rock on which the entire community of the faithful is erected. The Muslim state, with Muhammad at its head, predates the collection of the Hadith (narrations about the life of Muhammad) and the writing of the Quran itself. In Islam, it is not the religious message that promotes the faith into the halls of political power as in Judaism and Christianity, it is an original state of political and military strength that promotes the religious message.

Looked at this way, jihad is not a secondary concept in the development of Islam—something grafted onto the original religious message—rather it is the very origin of Islam, the sine qua non of the faith.

This furthermore explains the inability of Islamic culture to adapt and accept ideas of modernity and secular government. It is no secret that representative democracy does not take well in the Muslim world. Liberal democracy of the American variety requires the embrace of tolerance over truth, the relinquishment of any binding central religious truth or ideology in government. The very idea of our country arises out of a weariness of the religious wars of Europe. This idea, of a government without a religious vision of absolute truth, is contrary to the Muslim community's very conception of religious community.

An Intellectual Challenge

And herein lies the keystone of our problems. The attacks of Sept. 11 have created not only a military and economic challenge, but an intellectual one as well. Our dearly held idea of religious tolerance is confronted by a religion that seems at its root, incapable of it. Islam has never existed without the Islamic state, the Caliphate, and it would be hard-pressed to do so now. To accomplish a true secularization of the Muslim world would be to ignore the meaning of the Quran at the core—or at least as it is now interpreted by the most passionate believers.

Of course, the untangling of the religious from the political in Islam and the creation of a successful secular Islamic state is not an impossible task. In the years following World War I the Islamic Ottoman Empire eventually became the modern secular state of Turkey, following the reforms of Kumal Ataturk. The metamorphosis required inspired leadership, the deliberate and forceful confinement of Islam to the mosque and the home and the continued vigilance of the Turkish secular government. And other Islamic states have made varying degrees of progress away from theocracy.

The problem is that—as the experience of the West proves—the transformation of Islamic societies into ones that accept, to whatever degree, the separation of church and state will take time. After Sept. 11, time seems to be running out. And so certain painful questions must be confronted. Can the world truly continue to tolerate medieval minds with access to 21st century military hardware? Is there really room in the family of world faiths for a religious vision that is terrorist-prone, modernity-proof, plagued by fanaticism and susceptible to the hellish clarion call of jihad?

> "*Most Muslims are quick to say that extremists are distorting their faith— indeed, violating its fundamental principles of peace and justice—for political gains.*"

Islam Does Not Justify Terrorism

Teresa Watanabe

The September 11, 2001, terrorist attacks on America, which were carried out by professed Muslims, caused many to question whether the Islamic religion supported or promoted terrorism. In the following viewpoint journalist Teresa Watanabe draws on the opinions of several Islamic scholars in examining the question of whether Islam justifies violence and terrorism. The authorities she cites argue that while Islam's sacred texts include references to war and violence, nothing in Islam justifies acts such as the September 11 attacks. They claim that the terrorists are extremists who do not correctly represent Islamic views, and that Islam is no more inherently violent than Christianity or other religions. Watanabe is a religion writer for the *Los Angeles Times*.

As you read, consider the following questions:
1. What are some of the images associated with Islam, according to Watanabe?
2. Why are Islamic texts filled with militant verses, according to the author?
3. What criticisms are made about how extremists such as Osama bin Laden cite Koranic verses, according to Watanabe?

W hat kind of religion *is* this? How can Islam be used to justify both peace and war?

The recent terrorist attacks [on September 11, 2001], which authorities have blamed on Islamic extremists, have jolted Americans into asking questions about a religion that most non-Muslims still poorly understand. Islam, the faith of 1 billion people around the globe, has produced world empires, a civilization of stunning beauty and a theology of peace and submission to God.

But Islam also is plagued with images of ruthless Jihadi warriors, chopped-off hands, forced conversions—and now, hijacked airplanes blasting into the World Trade Center and Pentagon.

Distorting the Faith

Most Muslims are quick to say that extremists are distorting their faith—indeed, violating its fundamental principles of peace and justice—for political gains. Hamid Dabashi, chairman of the Middle Eastern languages and culture department at Columbia University, said Islam is no more inherently violent than Christianity, which produced followers who carried out brutal campaigns of extermination during the Crusades and the Inquisition.

"Nothing in the Koran, Islamic theology or Islamic law in any way, shape or form justifies ramming two airliners into civilian buildings," Dabashi said. "In every great religious tradition, you can launch the most humanistic, loving ideas, or the most violent terrorist actions."

References to War

But Dabashi and other experts said the Islamic religious texts lend themselves to manipulation by extremists because they are filled with fiery references to war, exhortations to fight oppression and mandates to mobilize against the enemy.

In the Koran's ninth chapter and fifth verse, for instance, Muslims are exhorted to "fight and slay The Pagans wherever ye find them. And seize them and beleaguer them and lie in wait for them . . ." (The passage also instructs that Muslims must embrace those who repent, "for Allah is Oft-Forgiving, Most Merciful." And, in other verses, Christians and Jews explicitly are exempted from attack, embraced as kindred "people of the book" qualified for paradise.)

A Product of the Times

The militant verses are a product of the times in which the faith emerged in the Arabian desert more than 1,400 years ago. The leading city of Mecca was in chaos, with drunken orgies, a scarcity of goods, political deadlock and a prevailing religion of animistic polytheism, according to world religions scholar Huston Smith.

The man who later would be called the prophet of God and challenge the Meccan corruption was born about 570, orphaned at an early age and named Muhammad—"the highly praised." He is regarded as a descendant of Ishmael, linking Islam with Judaism and Christianity as one of the three great monotheistic faiths stemming from Abraham, Ishmael's father.

Muhammad became a trader known for his honesty and integrity. He was a believer in one God and would often retire to a cave to meditate. At about age 40, the event that would change the world occurred: The angel Gabriel is said to have visited him while he was meditating, told him that God had chosen him as a messenger and revealed to him the first few words of the Koran.

Over the next several years, Muslims believe, the entire holy book would be revealed to Muhammad and form the scriptural basis of the faith, along with a collection of more than 60,000 accounts of the prophet's words and actions, known as "hadith."

In a climate of widespread inequity and idolatry, Islam was a revolutionary message of equality, justice and peace. It also featured several militant scriptures—particularly after Muhammad moved to Medina to escape a death plot hatched against him by the Meccan elites in 622. For the last 10 years of his life, he and his band of Muslims battled relentlessly to establish their faith against the Meccan establishment and other Arab tribes. The Koran and hadith reflect their environment, with numerous verses urging them to fight for Allah.

"Islam naturally includes a lot more material in its most classic, basic sources that are militant because that is the world they lived in—a world of successful military campaigns," said Reuven Firestone, a professor of medieval Judaism and Islam at Hebrew Union College in Los Angeles.

Terrorists Ignore Rules of Engagement

The Islamic sacred texts not only include exhortations to fight, they also lay out detailed rules of engagement. Experts say the terrorists broke every rule in the Islamic sacred books. The tradition expressly prohibits the killing of noncombatants: women, children, the aged, hermits, even trees. It forbids suicide. It even requires notice before attack.

Sheikh Yusuf Al-Qaradawi of Qatar, in a condemnation of the attacks as a "grave sin," cited a hadith in which Muhammad sees a woman killed in the battlefield and condemns the action. The Egyptian-born Qaradawi, one of Islam's most influential clerics, also said that even if the terrorists were driven by anger over the Palestinian-Israeli conflict, it was not permissible in Islam to shift the confrontation outside the region.

The Face of Terror Is Not the Face of Islam

These acts of violence [on September 11, 2001] against innocents violate the fundamental tenets of the Islamic faith. And it's important for my fellow Americans to understand that.

The English translation is not as eloquent as the original Arabic, but let me quote from the Koran itself: In the long run, evil in the extreme will be the end of those who do evil. For that they rejected the signs of Allah and held them up to ridicule.

The face of terror is not the true faith of Islam. That's not what Islam is all about. Islam is peace. These terrorists don't represent peace. They represent evil and war.

George W. Bush, remarks at the Islamic Center of Washington, DC, September 17, 2001.

The Islamic rules of engagement, however, seem to be lost on the terrorists. Khaled Abou El Fadl, University of California, Los Angeles, acting professor of Islamic law, has analyzed the religious references used in the literature and speeches of extremists, including a year-old interview with [terrorist] Osama bin Laden rebroadcast [in September 2001] on an Arabic TV channel.

He said bin Laden heavily focused on the Koranic verses about fighting oppression, and asked, "What greater oppression is there than the American imperialist forces within driving distance of the Holy Shrines?" That was a reference to U.S. forces that have been stationed in Saudi Arabia since the [1991] Persian Gulf War. Bin Laden told the interviewer from Al Jazeera network that the Holy Shrines were under occupation by infidel forces who were spreading AIDS in the Holy Land, and cited Koranic verses conveying God's permission for victims of injustice to throw off the yoke of oppression, according to Abou El Fadl.

The extremist leader appears to have memorized several Koranic verses, and cited them selectively and incompletely, but with calm and confidence, Abou El Fadl said. In the interview, bin Laden dismissed as inauthentic the more spiritual Islamic traditions that the highest jihad is an internal struggle to purify the soul, not a fight against unbelievers. When the interviewer presented him with opinions by Muslim jurists against killing noncombatants, he implied they had been co-opted by corrupt governments, Abou El Fadl said.

And when bin Laden cited a Koranic verse about fighting infidels, he left out the part requiring Muslims to seek peace if opponents do. Abou El Fadl said all Islamic scriptures on waging war are tempered by the command not to commit transgressions, but extremists ignore it.

"Unless you know the Koran, you will not be able to say, 'Wait a minute, where's the rest?'" Abou El Fadl said. "Bin Laden speaks in a way that if you're not already steeped in the tradition you would not think that there was any other possible interpretation. You're talking about an aura."

The UCLA scholar, who has written extensively on extremism and personally debated radicals growing up in the Middle East, said their common justification is that Islam is so endangered that the war to save it must be won by any means. Only after that, these radicals suggest, can Islamic ideals of mercy and justice be applied, Abou El Fadl said.

A Red Herring

Columbia University's Dabashi said that examining religion as a factor in terrorism was a red herring, as extremists are waging a political struggle against the perceived effects of colonialism simply veiled in the language of God. But Abou El Fadl disagreed.

"Of course religion influences this," Abou El Fadl said. "It gives you a sense of empowerment, entitlement and self-righteousness.

"Extremist theology," he added, "is a combustible brew of puritanism, ethical and moral irresponsibility and rampant apologetics."

| *"The bromides of American intellectuals wishing to sanitize* jihad*'s grotesque, barbarous reality will not save the life of a single potential victim."*

The Islamic Doctrine of Jihad Advocates Violence

John Perazzo

The literal meaning of the Arabic word *jihad* is "struggle." Some people have translated the word to mean "holy war" in order to expand Muslim territory and influence, and have argued that extremist Muslims are waging such a war against the United States and other non-Islamic countries. John Perazzo argues for such an understanding of jihad in the following viewpoint. He asserts that following the September 11, 2001, terrorist attacks, in which thousands of people were killed in New York and Washington, D.C., many church bodies and academics spread false notions of what jihad means in trying to argue that Islam is a "religion of peace." He argues that such views amount to wishful thinking and that many people in the Middle East and the Islamic world have embraced the extremely violent definition of jihad as an armed struggle against nonbelievers. Perazzo is the author of *The Myths That Divide Us: How Lies Have Poisoned American Race Relations.*

As you read, consider the following questions:

1. What did many churches and religious organizations say about Islam and jihad following the September 11 attacks, according to Perazzo?
2. What has jihad meant for most of Islam's history, according to the author?

John Perazzo, "The Meaning of Jihad," www.frontpagemagazine.com, November 26, 2002. Copyright © 2002 by the Center for the Study of Popular Culture. Reproduced by permission.

During the months following the 9-11 [2001] attacks—while the smoldering rubble left behind by the *jihad* warriors was still being sifted for human remains—the American public was reminded daily, by a multitude of purported experts, not only about Islam's status as a "religion of peace," but more particularly about the supposedly amiable nature of true *jihad* as well.

Church Pronouncements

Churches and religious organizations were among the most passionate in promoting the idea of peaceful *jihad*. Just days after 9-11, the Presbyterian News Service issued a press release explaining that for most Muslims, "*jihad* refers primarily to the inner struggle of being a person of virtue and submission to Allah in all aspects of life. This is sometimes described as '*jihad* of the heart.'" Along these lines, the Reverend Stephen Van Kuiken of Mt. Auburn Presbyterian Church in Cincinnati asserted, "The term *jihad* is often distorted to mean 'holy war,' but it has a deeper meaning . . . the struggle with our own selves. Literally, it means, 'exertion' or 'to struggle.' It means spiritual warfare, to battle with one's own demons in order to give ourselves over to God, in order to place ourselves in 'the arms of the wind.'"

Similarly, the United Church of Christ in Vancouver, Washington produced a publication stating that *jihad* means "to strive or to exert oneself," and that equating it with "holy war" is to "distort its spiritual significance and connotation." *Jihad*'s intent, the piece continued, is to establish "equilibrium within the inner being of man as well as in the human society in which that person functions." In its essence, *jihad* is "a reflection of Divine Justice and a necessary condition for peace in the human domain."

The National Council of Churches weighed in by explaining that "*jihad* means struggle or exertion in the way of God. The 'greater *jihad*' is the struggle against temptation and evil within oneself. The 'lesser *jihad*' is working against injustice or oppression in society."

Religious scholar and professor Dr. John Kaltner, who authored the 1999 book *Ishmael Instructs Isaac: An Introduction to the Qur'an for Bible Readers*, said he was troubled by "the manner in which many non-Muslims understand the term *jihad.*" The word, he said, "comes from an Arabic root whose primary sense refers to the act of putting forth effort to achieve some objective, [such as] the effort each person must exert in order to live his or her life as a good Muslim and avoid the temptation to sin." The only circumstances under which *jihad* permits open warfare, he said, is "when it is a defensive response to an attack." This definition was echoed by the Council on American-Islamic Relations' depiction of *jihad* as "the struggle against evil inclinations within oneself [and] the quality of life in society"—a struggle that may be taken to the battlefield solely for purposes of self-defense.

The axiom that *jihad* resorts to violence only to ward off aggressors suggests, of course, that it is rooted in a desire to maintain a state of justice or peace that is being threatened by external forces; in short, that it stems from an impulse to protect what is good, rather than from hateful bigotry or the ambition to overrun others. In this view, evil rests not in the violence of *jihadists*, but in whoever allegedly *caused* them to become violent. Proceeding from that premise, the executive director of the Alliance of Baptists asserted that the environment leading to the 9-11 attacks was created by American foreign policy—most notably its support for Israeli "violence."

Similarly, the Christian Methodist Episcopal Church's College of Bishops attributed the attacks to American "foreign policies around the world.". . .

The views of these religious organizations were echoed widely throughout academia as well. Harvard dean Michael Shinagel, for instance, publicly stated that *jihad*—far from having militant connotations—denotes instead one's personal quest "to promote justice and understanding in ourselves and in our society." As Middle East Forum director Daniel Pipes points out, Shinagel's benign depiction of *jihad* "reflect[s] the consensus of Islamic specialists" at universities all over this country. Pipes' careful study of the public statements of these professors shows that they view *jihad* largely as a "struggle without arms"—to do God's will, to improve one's own character, to resist worldly temptations, and to work for social justice.

Obviously many organizations—among them al-Qaeda,

Hamas, Islamic Jihad, Hezbollah, the Islamic Salvation Front, the Group Islamic Army, the al-Aqsa Martyrs Brigades, the Popular Front for the Liberation of Palestine, and the International Islamic Front for the Jihad Against Jews and Crusade[rs]—haven't yet been enlightened by the likes of American religious and academic experts, who presumably could set them straight about *jihad*'s "true, peaceful nature" that rejects violence except where absolutely necessary. How many slaughtered innocents might still be alive today, if only such warriors had understood *jihad* to mean what our priests, ministers, and professors claim it means?

Wishful Thinking

Self-deception and wishful thinking will not save us. The bromides of American intellectuals wishing to sanitize *jihad*'s grotesque, barbarous reality will not save the life of a single potential victim. For sadly, their platitudes have nothing remotely to do with reality. As Dr. Pipes explains, "the way the [militant] *jihadists* understand the term is in keeping with its usage through fourteen centuries of Islamic history"—during which it has meant the compulsory effort to forcibly expand Muslim territory and influence. "The goal is boldly offensive," says Pipes, "and its ultimate intent is nothing less than to achieve Muslim dominion over the entire world." Indeed the scholar Bat Ye'or explains that historically *jihad* has meant "war, dispossession, slavery, and death" for its victims. This is a far cry from the purported, noble struggle to "give oneself over to God."

If we wish to understand the true nature of *jihad*, we can learn a great deal from listening to the manner in which its actual practitioners and mouthpieces use the word, rather than the smiley-faced version that our religious leaders and college professors paint for us. For instance, the Middle East Media Research Institute (MEMRI) reports that during a November 8, 2002 sermon in a Baghdad mosque, an Iraqi cleric made the following remarks, which were broadcast by Iraqi TV: "We challenge [President (George W.) Bush and the Americans] with our words, before challenging [them] with our weapons. . . . We are patient . . . and we will fight them with all kinds of weapons. *Jihad, Jihad, Jihad, Jihad.* . . .

Jihad for the cause of Allah. . . . *Jihad* has become an obligation of every individual Muslim." He then exhorted all Muslims to "welcome death, welcome martyrdom for the cause for Allah."

A Rallying Slogan

In spite of the wide variety of interpretations given to *jihad* in modern times, some of which are soft and subtle, it is evident that the Muslim radicals . . . are uncompromisingly dedicated to the violent brand thereof. They refer to many Qur'anic passages which assure the martyr (that is, the dead in the course of *jihad*), all manner of rewards in the next world.

This is the reason why *jihad* has become the rallying slogan of many of those radical movements, as in 'Allah is the goal, the Prophet the model, the Qur'an the Constitution, Jihad the path, and death for the cause of Allah the most sublime creed'. Death in the course of *jihad* becomes, then, an expected and even desirable outcome.

Raphael Israeli, *Terrorism and Political Violence*, Autumn 1997.

"Oh Allah," the same cleric continued, "let the infidels fight each other, and dry their blood in their veins. Send Your soldiers against them. . . . destroy their fleet and their weapons; fight their soldiers . . . make them prey to the Muslims; Allah avenge Muslims' blood from them. . . . Oh Allah, for Thee we fight, we kill and are killed." This hardly sounds like a "struggle without arms."

According to MEMRI, a recent issue of the online magazine *Al-Ansar*, which has ties to al-Qaeda, wrote that "the importance of the human effort to annihilate the infidels . . . is what Allah sought to teach the Muslims. . . . *Jihad* is the way of torturing [the infidels] at our hands . . . with killing." Presumably the publishers of such rhetoric have not been fortunate enough to hear, as we Americans have, that *jihad* is in fact a peaceful pursuit. Equally unfortunate is the imam of the Great Mosque at King Saud University in Al-Riyadh, who lauds *jihad* as "the industry of death" taught by the prophet Muhammad.

MEMRI reports many additional Middle Eastern rantings about a *jihad* that looks nothing like the one in our apologists' fairy tales. The Saudi ambassador to London, for example, praises *jihadists* who become suicide bombers—on the grounds that "in the Koran . . . it is written that anyone who dies for the sake of Allah is a martyr." "The day of *jihad*," he says, "is the day of blood." A columnist for the Saudi government-controlled daily *Al-Jazirah* applauds suicide bombers for their "willingness to [wage] *jihad*." The foremost Egyptian cleric of Al Azhar University recently exhorted Palestinians to intensify their suicide attacks against Israeli women and children, characterizing such acts as the highest form of *jihad* operations. . . .

This is the *jihad* from which Western intellectuals wish to shield us with their cheerful tales of people struggling "to promote justice and understanding." This is the authentic, hideous face of *jihad* recognized throughout the Islamic world—and preached passionately by many of its most eminent religious leaders. Because such clerics embrace and endorse the concept of militant *jihad*, it is not surprising that ever-greater numbers of young Arabs are volunteering to become "holy warriors"—that is, suicide bombers. . . .

And so it goes, as aspiring *jihadists* line up for an opportunity to murder and thereby glorify God—not only making a mockery of our politically correct definitions of *jihad*, but more importantly, preventing us from truly understanding the enemy we face.

"The 'holy war' concept, for which many non-Muslims use the word Jihad, is foreign to Islam."

The Islamic Doctrine of Jihad Does Not Advocate Violence

Javeed Akhter

Javeed Akhter is executive director of the International Strategy and Policy Institute, an organization that publishes books and conducts public discussions on issues relating to Islam in America. He is also the author of *The Seven Phases of the Prophet Muhammad's Life*. In the following viewpoint, he defends Islam from charges that it endorses violence against non-Muslims. In particular, he argues against the concept of Islamic jihad as a "holy war" waged to kill all infidels. The concept of jihad, he argues, can be used to justify defensive and disciplined warfare, but its greater meaning is to struggle with one's inner self to achieve spiritual goals. The concept of "holy war" is foreign to Islam, he concludes.

As you read, consider the following questions:

1. What sorts of charges have been made against Islam by conservative Christian commentators, according to Akhter?
2. What advice does the author provide about reading and interpreting the Koran?
3. What comparisons does Akhter make between crusade and jihad?

Javeed Akhter, "Does Islam Promote Violence?" www.ispi-usa.org, August 20, 2002. Copyright © 2002 by the International Strategy and Policy Institute. Reproduced by permission.

The evangelist Franklin Graham and the conservative Christian commentator Pat Robertson's assertion that Islam exhorts its followers to be violent against non-Muslims, are only two of the most prominent voices that are part of a rising cacophony of vicious criticism of the Qur'an. One can read and hear a whole range of negative opinions about this issue in the media. Few have taken an in depth look at the issue. What does the Qur'an actually say about violence against non-Muslims? Does it say what Robertson and Graham claim it does? Does it say that it is the religious duty of Muslims to kill infidels? But first some basic principles about reading and understanding the Qur'an. After all studying the Qur'an is not exactly like reading Harry Potter. Like any other scripture there are rules that may be followed for a proper understanding of the text.

Principles for Understanding the Qur'an

Muslim scholars suggest that those who read the Qur'an should keep at a minimum the following principles in mind. First the reader should have an awareness of the inner coherence in the Qur'an. As the verses are connected to each other the reader should study at the least the preceding and following verses for a sense of the immediate context. Also the reader should look at all of the verses that deal with the same subject in the book. These are frequently scattered all over the scripture. The indices provided in many of the exegeses of the Qur'an as well as the books of concordance allow the reader to get this information relatively easily. Often there is information available about the occasion of revelation, the historical context, of a particular verse. This requires at least a cursory knowledge of Prophet Muhammad's life. As Professor Fazlur Rahman of the University of Chicago would frequently point out, the Qur'an, in part at least, may be looked upon as a running commentary on the mission of Prophet Muhammad. Finally Qur'anic scholars advise us to analyze the way Prophet implemented a particular directive in a verse of the Qur'an in his own life and ministry. For all Muslims Prophet Muhammad was the ultimate exemplar of the Qur'an and its living embodiment.

Let us examine the verses in question with these exegetical principles in mind. One of the verses says "put down the polytheists wherever you find them, and capture them and beleaguer them and lie in wait for them at every ambush" (Koran 9:5). The immediate context, as Muhammad Asad (*The Message of the Qur'an*) points out, is that of a "war in progress" and not a general directive. It was an attempt to motivate Muslims in self-defense.

Understanding Jihad

Since Sept. 11 [2001] the media have more than ever been tossing about the word jihad. The word does not mean "holy war"; it means "to strive" or "to struggle." According to the teachings of Islam, our greatest enemy is within us. In Arabic this force is referred to as the nafs—"ego," if you will—that part of us that is led by our greed and arrogance, rather than the inner-self that God created in order that it might worship him and bring a sense of balance, peace and justice to the world.

The Koran tells Muslims to join the struggle (that is to say, to make jihad) against that which is evil and to enjoin what is good and just, with God as their guide. Writings by Islamic scholars throughout the centuries have listed four types of jihad:

1. jihad of the heart, which leads the struggle against temptations and the evil within, so that one may comply with God's will and be pure of heart.

2. jihad of the tongue, in which one uses the power of speech to enjoin that which is good and forbid that which is evil.

3. jihad of the hand, in which Muslims use their actions to defend the weak from the oppressor and to work toward bringing about a just world.

4. jihad of the sword, or combat, which is the last resort. Jihad of the sword is not always a military struggle. It also includes the use of political or diplomatic means.

Karima Diane Alavi, *America*, March 4, 2002.

Muslims were given permission to defend themselves around the time of Prophet Muhammad's migration from Makkah, where he grew up, to the city of Madinah where he spent the rest of his life. This occurred in the 13th year of his 23-year mission. The danger to Muslims in Makkah at this time was extreme and there was a real possibility of their total eradication. They were permitted to fight back in self-defensc against those who violently oppressed them. "Permission is given (to fight) those who have taken up arms against you wrongfully. And verily God (Allah) is well able to give you succor. To those who have been driven forth from their homes for no reason than this that say 'Our Lord is God.'" Qur'an goes on to add, "Hath not God repelled some men by others, cloisters and churches and synagogues and mosques, wherein the name of God is ever mentioned, would assuredly have been pulled down." (Qur'an 22: 39–42)

On another occasion Qur'an says, "Fight in the cause of God those who fight you, but don't transgress limits; for God loves not the transgressor."

The verse goes on to say "And fight them on until there is no more oppression, and there prevail justice and faith in God; but if they cease let there be no hostility except to those who practice oppression." (Qur'an 2: 190–193)

Muslim scholars are of the opinion that war is permitted in self-defense, when other nations have attacked an Islamic state, or if another state is oppressing a section of its own people. When Muslims were to fight a war they had to maintain great discipline, avoiding injury to the innocent and use only the minimum force needed. Striking a blow in anger, even in battle, was prohibited. The prisoners of war were to be treated in a humane fashion. However this is only a part of Jihad that Muslims are allowed to practice.

A greater Jihad is struggle against one's own inner self.

Jihad and Internal Struggle

The word Jihad comes from the root letters JHD, which means to struggle or to strive. It is understood by piety minded Muslims as a positive, noble and laudatory term. That is how most apply it in their personal, social, political and military lives. The history of the Muslims rulers, on the other hand, gives us examples of those who attempted to sanctify their wars of personal aggrandizement as wars for a noble cause by applying the label Jihad to them. A few even named their war departments as the departments of Jihad. This kind of behavior may be likened to a politician's attempt to wrap him in the flag. Such exploitation of the term should not be allowed to corrupt the original or the commonly understood meaning of the word, which is to strive for the highest possible goals, struggle against injustice and practice self denial and self control to achieve the moral purity to which all piety minded people aspire.

The "holy war" concept, for which many non-Muslims use the word Jihad, is foreign to Islam. Rather, it comes from a concept first used to justify the Crusades by the Christian Church during the Middle Ages. The concept of "holy war" may even go back to the time when the emperor Constantine the Great allegedly saw a vision in the sky with the inscription on the cross, "in hoc signo vinces" (in this sign you will be the victor). The Arabic term, as has been pointed out by scholars, for "the holy war" would be al-harab al-muqaddas, which neither appears in the Qur'an or the sayings of the Prophet Muhammad (Hadith). Prophet Muhammad's wars were defensive wars against groups who sought to eradicate Islam and the Muslims.

It is interesting and useful for social scientists or philologists to study how the meaning and usage of words differ in different communities. Ironically the word "crusade", because of its association with the Crusades in the Middle Ages, should have had a pejorative sense to it and yet the word has acquired an ennobled meaning in the West. This in spite of the fact that the Church itself, along with most historians, acknowledge the injustice of the Crusades and the atrocities done in the name of faith. On the other hand, the word "Jihad" which means for Muslims, striving for the highest possible goal, has acquired the negative connotation of the holy war.

It is clear from even a cursory study of the Qur'an that Islam does not permit, condone or promote violence. Just the opposite, it abhors violence and allows it only in self-defense. A claim to the contrary is no more than bad fiction.

The critics of the Qur'an should remember that if the Bible were similarly quoted out of context it would appear to be an extraordinarily violent scripture. I will leave Graham and Robertson to defend the violence in the Bible and the history of Christianity.

"We were assaulted [on September 11, 2001] by Wahhabis engaged, as they always are, in the pursuit of . . . holy war."

The Wahhabist Strain of Islamic Fundamentalism Supports Terrorism

Patrick Lang

Patrick Lang, a retired army colonel, served as chief Middle East analyst for the U.S. Defense Intelligence Agency during the 1990s. In the following viewpoint he describes the origins and development of Wahhabism—a fundamentalist Islamic movement that began in the 1800s in what is now Saudi Arabia. This particular sect of Islam, Lang writes, espouses a strict observance of Islamic law and condemns all other Muslims as heretics. Lang writes that Wahhabi Muslims believe that the Western world is corrupt and the United States is the "Great Satan." Such beliefs inspire terrorism, including the September 11, 2001, attacks, Lang writes, and should not be overlooked in America's war against terrorism.

As you read, consider the following questions:

1. What practical reasons did President George W. Bush have for arguing that the September 11 attacks were carried out by people who "hijacked Islam," according to Lang?
2. How did Wahhabism develop in Saudi Arabia, as described by the author?
3. What does Lang find disturbing about American mosques?

S ince the heinous attacks on the World Trade Center in New York and the Pentagon on Sept. 11, 2001, the Bush administration has issued an unending stream of statements informing us that these barbarous crimes were committed by people who embrace a "perverted version of Islam" or by those who have "hijacked Islam." It is also often assumed that Islam is a religion of gentleness and peaceful behavior and that no true Muslim would commit such acts. From the Bush administration's point of view, it is undoubtedly necessary to generalize in this way, no matter what the truth may be. Coalitions must be built and maintained across the world, and Muslim allies or partners must be made to feel that they are not condemned en masse with the killers.

But generalizations are always defective in some way, and this generalization about the nature of the faith and culture of more than a billion people is massively defective and a burden to sound analysis of the actual threat facing the United States.

War and Nonviolence in Islam

It is true that ordinary Muslims seek to live in peace with their neighbors. Their Scriptures and traditions oppose the kinds of behavior that killed so many on Sept. 11. The Quran forbids suicide, as it forbids war made upon women, children and the innocent. Nevertheless, the impression has been created that Islam is a pacifist religion, rather like the 21st-century Christianity that has all but abandoned the traditional Christian doctrine of the just war. In fact, Islam is not a pacifist religion. It has never been a pacifist religion. The Prophet Muhammad led his armies in person against the enemies of the emergent Islamic revelation. His successors (caliphs) did the same in the early days of Islamic expansion. The Caliph Omar himself accepted the surrender of Jerusalem when it was captured from the Byzantines.

Nevertheless, it is true that the Islamic tradition contains within it humane attitudes toward life and a spirit of benevolence toward all mankind. This tendency is most clearly found in the mystic Sufi orders, to which a great many Muslims belong. A recent statement by Prince Hassan of Jordan, himself a member of the Naqshbandi Order, offers an example of the thinking typical of the Sufi element in Islam. "Respecting the sanctity of life is the cornerstone of all great faiths" the prince said. "Such acts of extreme violence, in which innocent men, women and children are both the targets and the pawns, are totally unjustifiable. No religious tradition can or will tolerate such behavior and all will loudly condemn it." If this is the thinking of a prominent Muslim, indeed a lineal descendant of the Prophet Muhammad himself, then who is it that attacked us?

The answer is that we were attacked by those who hold the Sufis and most ordinary Muslims in contempt as not really Islamic at all. We were attacked by those who have always been prepared to kill if they could not persuade. We were assaulted by Wahhabis engaged, as they always are, in the pursuit of the central element of their belief, the jihad or holy war.

Wahhabism and the Saudi Kingdom

Sunni Islam, the majority Islamic faith, is a religion of laws, of legal schools and jurisprudence. For Sunnis, God has made law for humanity to live. There are four great schools of the religious law in Sunni Islam. One of these schools is named for Ibn Hanbal (A.D. 780–855), who believed that the law should be seen in a very "boiled down," literalist way that leaves little room for interpretation, adaptation or concessions to modernity.

The Hanbali school of law would probably have died out, discarded by believers as too extreme for "real life," except for an 18th-century scholar named Muhammad Abd al-Wahhab, who lived in what is now Saudi Arabia. Abd al-Wahhab embraced Ibn Hanbal's ideas and convinced a desert chieftain named Ibn Sa'ud to accept his version of Hanbalism as the official faith of what eventually became Saudi Arabia. This faith, popularly known as Wahhabism, rejected the right of all other Muslims to believe and practice Islam in their own ways. It particularly condemned Sufi brotherhoods for their attempts to experience God personally rather than through the rigid observance of Islamic law.

Wahhabism continues to condemn all other Muslims. It cites the Quran's description of war made against unbelievers in the first centuries of Islam to justify, indeed to demand, unceasing war to the death against other less observant Muslims and especially against non-Muslim unbelievers. This war against the "infidels" is the jihad, a moral obligation of every true Muslim. The Wahhabis, however, insist on an understanding of jihad that other Muslims have long since left behind. For the great majority of "the faithful," jihad has long been divided into the "Greater Jihad" and the "Lesser Jihad." The lesser jihad is the jihad of war, death and blood. The greater jihad is the inner struggle of every pious Muslim to bring himself closer to God through self-denial, charity and a moral life. This was not, and is not, the Wahhabi way. For them, the unbeliever, including non-Wahhabi Muslims, must accept their view of orthodox religious practice or suffer the consequences.

The early followers of this sect, generally condemned in their day as heretics by other Sunni, did their best to spread their rule by force across the Arabian Peninsula until in the late 18th century the Ottoman Turkish governor of Egypt sent his army into the area and utterly crushed them. From that time until the creation of modern Saudi Arabia at the beginning of the 20th century, Wahhabism was a little-known offshoot of Islam. At that time, Abd al-Aziz al-Sa'ud, the first king of Saudi Arabia, unified the Arabian Peninsula by force. By 1925, this process was largely completed. In the new Saudi state, Wahhabism was the official faith and the only one sanctioned by the state. To this day no Christian, Jewish or other religious establishment is allowed in the kingdom.

Wahhabi Missionary Expansion

In the early years of the Saudi state, the jihad doctrines of Wahhabism were ruthlessly enforced by the Ikhwan (Brotherhood) Bedouin armies which had brought the kingdom into being. The Ikhwan's treatment of other Bedouin tribes living in Iraq and Jordan illustrates their intolerance. Believing they had a divine mission, the Ikhwan tribes constantly raided those countries, crossing borders that had no meaning for them, to kill peaceful shepherds, their families and livestock. No quarter was ever given to women and children. Such unrestrained violence was an abomination both in Islamic tradition and Arab customary law (urf). The atrocities came to an end only when the governments of Iraq and Jordan adopted the tactic of pursuing the Ikhwan into Saudi Arabia to deal with them in 1922–25. The Saudi government then sought to disarm the Ikhwan tribes. This led to a revolt by the zealots, who denounced the king as "no true Muslim." The revolt was put down, and its leaders were executed.

Bin Laden Is a Fundamentalist

Whereas Professor [David F.] Forte sees the problem as a small group of active terrorists in al Qaeda, I see the entire fundamentalist movement constituting the problem. I hold that Islamic fundamentalists stand outside of historic Islam and are already within [Osama] bin Laden's extremist ranks.

To me, every fundamentalist Muslim, no matter how peaceable in his own behavior, is part of a murderous movement and is thus, in some fashion, a foot soldier in the war that bin Laden has launched against civilization. . . .

Sadly, I must report that the sympathizers of Osama bin Laden are legion. Fully one quarter of the populations in Pakistan and the Palestinian Authority (survey research finds, in separate polls both overseen by U.S. organizations) consider the September 11 [2001, terrorist] attacks acceptable according to the laws of Islam. To me, this suggests that a very substantial body of Muslim opinion is already in bin Laden's camp; more, that virtually the whole range of fundamentalist Islamic opinion agrees with his goals and his methods.

Daniel Pipes, *National Review*, October 22, 2001.

In the aftermath of the Ikhwan revolt, the Saudi government sought to moderate its policies and practices to make it possible to interact productively with the outside world. The Saudi government has followed this path of relative moderation ever since. Saudi moderation became particularly important after the discovery of huge deposits of petroleum in the kingdom before the Second World War. A kind of alliance with the United States in that war created a relationship that, although it has never been formalized by treaty, has stood the test of time. In fact, the relationship cannot be formalized, because Wahhabism does not allow such a relationship with a non-Muslim state. While the Saudi government has pursued its long-term alignment with the United States, very different currents have run beneath the surface of Saudi society.

The al-Sa'ud royal family created the kingdom by force. Its members are descended from desert warlords of the central peninsula. They are not descended from the Prophet Muhammad, as are the kings of Jordan and Morocco. In their subjects' eyes, their continued legitimacy derives from their support and adherence to Wahhabi Islam. Because of this, it has been very difficult for the royal government to restrict the teaching of Wahhabi doctrines in divinity schools and universities or to prevent the preaching of these doctrines in the country's mosques. It has also been impossible for the government to prevent the export of vast sums of private Saudi money to support Wahhabi missionary works abroad.

What kind of pious missionary works have they accomplished? Schools have been founded across the Islamic world, in Europe and the United States. Mosques have been built and endowed in many places. Sheikh Hisham Muhammad Kabbani, leader of the Islamic Supreme Council of America and an adversary of the Wahhabis, recently wrote to the State Department that because mosques in the United States are not regulated by the government as they are in the Islamic world, 80 per cent of U.S. mosques are endowed by Wahhabi groups and have prayer leaders selected by the same groups. As a consequence, the moral formation of American Muslim youth is in Wahhabi hands.

In the 1950's, President Gamal Abdel Nasser of Egypt suppressed the Society of the Muslim Brethren (the Ikhwan Muslimeen) and drove them underground. The Muslim Brethren were the oldest and the most murderous of Arab extremist groups. Soon thereafter private money from the oil-rich economies of the Persian Gulf "rescued" the brotherhood from extinction. In the decades since then, the Egyptian Muslim Brethren have become a worldwide network of Wahhabi/Ikhwan cells. They are one of the largest components of the Al Qaeda network created by Osama bin Laden [that was responsible for the September 11 attacks].

Self-Deception in the War on Terror

The Wahhabi/Ikhwan movement believes that the Islamic world is corrupt and that the West has corrupted it. They believe deeply that existing governments in their countries must be brought down to make way for a "pure" Islamic life. They believe that the United States is the ultimate enemy, "The Great Satan." They will do whatever is needed to eliminate the United States as an obstacle to their dreams.

It is against this backdrop of history and religious belief that the endlessly repeated protestations of spokesmen for the U.S. executive branch on the subject of Islam's "innocence" for 9/11 should be considered. Islam has never turned away from the medieval division of the world into believers and infidels. It has never done so because it has never experienced the equivalent of the Protestant Reformation and the Catholic Counter-Reformation, which eventually produced societies resigned to the necessity of mutual toleration. In the long history of Islam there have been any number of brave souls who sought to bring their faith to a similar "resignation." Their fate has been uniformly tragic.

The history of the Wahhabi/Ikhwan movement follows a cyclic pattern, in which periods of adaptation are fiercely resisted by waves of revivalist fighters determined to justify Islam with the sword. These jihadi fighters have never been and are not now the objects of anathema by most Islamic theologians and scholars. They are merely thought to be "extreme."

As a result we face a dangerous situation, in which the U.S. government considers the Wahhabi/Ikhwan jihadis to be Islamic heretics outside mainstream Islam, while the great majority of Muslim religious dignitaries here and abroad consider them to be only "misguided." President [George W.] Bush is undoubtedly correct when he says that we have a long road ahead of us in a fight against bitter enemies. We should ask ourselves if self-deception by U.S. policy makers concerning the nature of those enemies is not more of a handicap than we should impose on leaders who are serious about the fight against global terrorism. Should not the war on terror follow the example of those Iraqi and Jordanian governments of the last century who pursued the Ikhwan jihadi into their lairs and forced the Saudi government to repress their violent activities?

"Mass terror is a . . . more egregious form of evil . . . [that] is outside of even militant Islamic fundamentalism."

Terrorism Is Not Supported by Any Form of Islamic Fundamentalism

David F. Forte

David F. Forte is a law professor at Cleveland State University and the author of *Studies in Islamic Law: Classical and Contemporary Applications*. In the following viewpoint he argues that the September 11, 2001, terrorist attacks that were perpetrated by Osama bin Laden's al-Qaeda organization constitute a perversion of all forms of Islam, including its Wahhabist and fundamentalist strains. While there is much that is objectionable about some strains of militant Islamic fundamentalism, he writes, Islam should not be blamed for the events of September 11. Osama bin Laden has become an enemy of Islam by changing it from a religion into a totalitarian political ideology. The United States should be careful to maintain a moral distinction between bin Laden's ideas and Islam, Forte concludes.

As you read, consider the following questions:
1. What public reaction to his arguments does Forte describe?
2. How is Osama bin Laden's version of Islam different from Wahhabism?
3. Why would the attitude that Islam is a religion of terror hamper America's war against terrorism, according to Forte?

L ast week [in October 2001], the Upper Sharia Court in Gwadabawa, Sokoto State, in northern Nigeria sentenced a 30-year-old pregnant woman to be stoned for premarital sex. Human-rights organizations immediately protested the sentence. The human-rights problems in imposing a 1,000-year-old codification of law are not confined to tribalistic Nigeria. Muslims and non-Muslims alike suffer under some of the extreme provisions of the Sharia (Islamic law) applied, directly or indirectly, in Egypt, Saudi Arabia, Pakistan, Iran, and other areas. But these actions are not the essentialist Islam. In fact, most contemporary fundamentalist impositions do not even observe the strict procedural protections the Sharia provided, and under which few if any of today's attacks on human rights could be accomplished. They violate the provisions of the very law they claim to be following. Furthermore, today's application of the criminal provisions of the Sharia are as ahistorical as they are problematical for human rights. The Islamic empire in its various forms more often substituted its own criminal courts and criminal decrees for that of the *qadi* (judge), leaving the criminal-law provisions of the Sharia among the least developed areas of classical Islamic law.

The legalistic element of Islam spans wide variations. Not all wish to impose the Sharia in all its archaic details. Many call for a new *ijtihad*, or redevelopment of the law from its sources to meet modern conditions. Nor is legalism the sole voice of Islam: From the beginning, rationalist, theological, and mystical traditions have vied with it. I believe that, like Christians and Jews, most Muslims crave a moral space in which to worship God and obtain forgiveness and salvation. The imposition of all the elements of a 1,000-year-old code of law would close up that space.

Yet as offensive to human rights and dignity as the stoning of a woman for an act of sexual immorality is, it is not the same as flying a plane into a building to kill thousands of innocent civilians. It is not the same as training thousands to destroy societies and impose political control over millions of people. Mass terror is a different and qualitatively more egregious form of evil. It is outside of even militant Islamic fundamentalism.

War Against Islam

Over the past few weeks [since the September 11, 2001, terrorist attacks], I have argued that [terrorist] Osama bin Laden and his Taliban allies represent a perversion of Islam and are engaged in a campaign to change Islam itself—to define the faith politically, and not primarily legally or theologically. The evidence, I believe, is unequivocal: His war is as much against Islam as it is against the West. I have written that Islam is a multivocal religion, that from its start it has debated within itself the nature of its identity. And I have noted that among all its varied traditions, one thing remains clear: The acts of the terrorists of September 11, and the justification of them by Osama bin Laden, replicate in modern guise a violent faction, the Kharajites, that Islam found totally anathema to the faith early in its history. In other writings, I have asserted that this form of extremism has been inspired by the writings of influential modernist radicals, such as Sayyid Qutb of Egypt, who believe that virtually all Islam is in a state of unbelief and needs to be reconquered. Thus, in its modern form, bin Laden's kind of extremism has much more in common with Stalin, Hitler, and Mao than it does with Islamic tradition. Like those state terrorists, bin Laden is at war with his own people. And finally, I have baldly asserted that bin Laden and his extremists are evil, pure and simple, and Islam is not.

Since these opinions have been aired, I have received many letters, telephone calls, and e-mails. Without exception, Muslims who have contacted me have been grateful for my views. They have been relieved to hear how a Christian and Westerner is explaining to Americans the true nature of their religion. They have thanked me for my understanding of Islam. They agree with my characterization of bin Laden and al Qaeda [the group responsible for the September 11 attacks].

But, Muslim opinion notwithstanding, some American columnists have insisted that I misunderstand Islam. . . .

[Writer] Andrew Sullivan thinks that bin Laden is much closer to the real Islam than I make him out to be. He accepts bin Laden's premise: We are in a religious war. More accurately, Sullivan wants us to be in a religious war, because

Sullivan himself wants to make war on religion until it learns to believe less in itself.

Sullivan has two themes. The first is that legalistic Islam, the Islam of the fundamentalists, has been making dramatic headway in the Muslim world. There's nothing new there. But his corollary—that bin Laden is only a prominent example of the fundamentalist movement (indeed, of all religious fundamentalism)—is dangerously awry. . . .

The Enemy of My Enemy

There is no doubt that the militant edge of Islamic fundamentalism has expanded in recent decades. Many scholars of Islam have delineated, in meticulous detail, the particular movements and leaders in various countries of the Muslim world. They have provided us, if we would but listen, with the knowledge by which to develop policies that can support genuinely religiously based reformist movements, free of the hate that is capable of undermining world peace and stability.

What's been missing from recent discussion is an acknowledgement that over the past decade, the United States has done little to discourage Islamic governments from appeasing radical Islamist movements within their nations. On the contrary, a kind of patronizing attitude towards Muslims—a view that Islam is dangerous, militant, and narrow-minded was not uncommon in our government's attitude, and particularly in our relations with countries such as the Sudan, Pakistan, and Afghanistan. In another forum, I noted three critical effects of that policy:

- If we don't believe in protecting people from religious persecution, we must be the materialist, bankrupt culture the Islamic radicals claim we are.
- If we allow, for reasons of state, that it's all right with us that Islamic governments give in to the radicals' tyrannical agenda, we acknowledge that radical Islam is a legitimate force in the world.
- If we in effect say that these issues are not human-rights problems, that they are "a Muslim problem," we treat our genuine Islamic friends with a patronizing indifference.

Such attitudes have only given the radicals more validation, increasing Muslims' contempt for the West. Those beliefs have largely reflected the views of religion in general held by the secular elites. . . . Fortunately for America and the world, theirs is an attitude President [George W.] Bush does not share.

Osama bin Laden and Wahhabism

Sullivan calls particular attention to the Saudi spread of its puritanical Wahhabist sect and its embrace of the most rigorous and narrow legal school in Islam. In addition, he points to Saudi support of *madrasas*, which he rightly describes as being often mere schools of hate, which do not advance prospects of peace and mutual acceptance.

Kallaugher. © 2001 by *The Economist*. Reproduced by permission of Cartoonists & Writers Syndicate.

But Osama bin Laden's version of Islam is different even from Wahhabism. And it certainly is different from more moderate forms of Islamic fundamentalism, let alone traditional Islam. Bin Laden's Islam has even gone beyond being a religious sect. It has become, like the Leninism[1] it in significant ways replicates, a political ideology. Even his calls to action are political war cries: the crusades, the land of the

1. named after Vladimir Lenin, Communist leader of the Soviet Union from 1918 to 1924

two holy mosques, the 80-year-old political betrayal of the Arabs. He would, and has, killed Muslims who disagree with his beliefs—or rather, with his need for control. He joyfully makes war on innocent civilians, war even the most passionate partisans of the Sharia have difficulty justifying. It is both ironic and revealing that Osama bin Laden, who makes use of the products of these Wahhabist schools, seeks to overthrow the Saudi regime itself.

Without being blind to the dangers of militant fundamentalism, we must remain aware of the moral distinction between sects like the Wahhabis and terrorist groups like al Qaeda and Islamic Jihad. It is a difference that the majority of Muslims, including many of those sympathetic to fundamentalism, are capable of affirming. However timorous Muslim spokesmen may salt their condemnation of the terrorists with formulaic denunciations of Israel, they all are aware of one truth: Bin Laden hates them and means to do them in. What we must do, at all costs, is to prevent bin Laden's call to arms from bringing Islamic fundamentalists into his extremist ranks and into his political battle. And our starting point must be a respect for the distinctions between the great varieties of Islamic tradition and the perversions of them. . . .

In sum, most Muslims and most Muslim leaders know emphatically what America's leaders and intellectuals must know: that extremists like bin Laden do not represent historic or mainstream Islam, not even in its most problematic forms. Bin Laden's extremism is meant to establish a brand of Islam after the pattern of Afghanistan. It follows the example of the extremist government of Sudan, which inflicts a terrorist war upon millions of Christians within its own borders. It undermines and attacks legal values most Muslims hold to be part of Islamic law. And it mocks any semblance of the toleration and peaceful coexistence that have marked much of Islamic history.

Perversely, by treating Islam as a religion of terror, Sullivan plays into bin Laden's strategy of presenting himself as a religious hero. The more accurate course is to brand bin Laden for what he is—an enemy to the peaceful and tolerant (and even some of the less-tolerant) traditions of Islam—and so isolate him from the faith of the multitudes he seeks to win over. If American policy were based on Sullivan's analysis, it would be grounded in a patronizing and distorted view of Islam (and religious faith in general), and raise a front of Muslim nations against the West into the bargain. War with the entire Islamic religion is as unnecessary as it is grossly imprudent. More importantly, by continuing to maintain that moral bright line between terrorism and Islam, we help to legitimate all the varied and peaceful traditions of Islam—including those that oppose fundamentalism. This permits us to precisely isolate and destroy the terrorists, while working on a multifaceted program to blunt and reduce militant fundamentalism within Islam.

Periodical Bibliography

The following articles have been selected to supplement the diverse views presented in this chapter.

Paul Berman	"The Philosopher of Terror," *New York Times Magazine*, March 23, 2003.
James A. Beverley	"Is Islam a Religion of Peace?" *Christianity Today*, January 7, 2002.
Ladan Boroumand and Roya Boroumand	"Terror, Islam, and Democracy," *Journal of Democracy*, April 2002.
Khaled Abou El Fadl	"Terrorism Is at Odds with Islamic Tradition," *Los Angeles Times*, August 22, 2001.
Jack Fischel	"The Road to September 11th," *Midstream*, February/March 2002.
Maureen Freely	"The Ignorance of Islamaphobes," *New Statesman*, December 17, 2001.
James Turner Johnson	"Jihad and Just War," *First Things*, June/July 2002.
John Kelsay	"Bin Laden's Reasons: Interpreting Islamic Tradition," *Christian Century*, February 27, 2002.
Paul Kurtz	"Religious Correctness and the Qur'an," *Free Inquiry*, Winter 2002.
Abdul Maseeh	"The Islamic Concept of Peace," *Free Inquiry*, Spring 2002.
A. Rashied Omar	"Islam and Violence," *Ecumenical Review*, April 2003.
Daniel Pipes	"Jihad and the Professors," *Commentary*, November 2002.
Salman Rushdie	"Yes, This Is About Islam," *New York Times*, November 2, 2001.
Nada El Sawy	"Yes, I Follow Islam, but I'm Not a Terrorist," *Newsweek*, October 15, 2001.
David Schafer	"Islam and Terrorism: A Humanist View," *Humanist*, May/June 2002.
Leon Wieseltier	"Washington Diarist: The Incoherence (Democracy, Islam, and Politics)," *New Republic*, October 29, 2001.

CHAPTER 3

What Is the Status of Women Under Islam?

Chapter Preface

From 1996 to the end of 2001, the country of Afghanistan was under the control of a regime called the Taliban—a word derived from Talib, or religious students. The Taliban leaders were mostly young Islamic scholars trained in madrassas (religious schools) located in Pakistan and funded in part by Saudi Arabia. They said they wanted to install a pure form of Islamic government in Afghanistan. To this end they enforced numerous rules that they said were based on classic Islamic teachings, banning, among other things, music, movies, picnics, wedding parties, mixed-sex gatherings, toys, cameras, cigarettes, alcohol, and most books.

The Taliban regime, citing Islamic law, also greatly restricted the rights and public roles of women. Female education, from kindergarten through graduate school, was abolished. Women were banned from seeking jobs or wearing makeup, and for the most part were kept within their homes. When out in public, the women were required to wear the burka, an all-encompassing garment that covers women from head to toe, with a small square of gauze to allow for vision. Punishments for breaking the Taliban's laws included imprisonment, flogging, or worse. Religious police, as part of the "Department for the Propagation of Virtue and the Suppression of Vice," constantly roamed the streets looking for women traveling without a male relative or otherwise breaking the rules, often summarily whipping those they found.

In part because of their treatment of women and their general human rights record, the Taliban were never formally recognized by the United States or the United Nations. But criticism of the Taliban's treatment of women came not only from Western nations and international institutions but from other Muslims who argued that the Taliban's laws and restrictions did not truly represent Islam. Hassan Hathout, an Islamic scholar and director of the outreach program at the Islamic Center of Southern California, argues that contrary to what the Taliban taught, women played prominent public roles at the time Islam was founded. "Women participated in public affairs, were involved in negotiating treaties, were even judges. Islam declared gender equality through the Prophet's words, 'Women are the siblings of men.'" Hathout and others argued that the Taliban's restrictions on women were a perversion of Islam.

The Taliban's reign over Afghanistan ended in late 2001 when the United States—in response to the September 11, 2001, terrorist attacks—attacked and deposed the regime because it had provided a base of operations for Osama bin Laden's terrorist network. In consequence, most of the restrictions on women's movements were lifted. However, debate continues within the Muslim world over the Taliban's treatment of women and whether it was indicative of the true nature of Islam. Many nations governed by Islamic law, such as Saudi Arabia, impose similar restrictions on women (although not as extreme as the Taliban). Feminist activist Azam Kamguian contends that Islam has "intrinsic hostility to equality between the sexes [and] to women's rights." Whether or not this is true is a fundamental question debated in the viewpoints in this chapter.

"Islam's psychotic obsession with female chastity, modesty and virginity has rendered men incapable of viewing women as equal and worthy companions."

Women Are Oppressed Under Islam

Voula

Voula is the author of the *Young People's Guide to Understanding Religion* and a member of the Atheist Foundation of Australia. In the following viewpoint she argues that Islam denigrates and oppresses women. She dismisses arguments that tradition and tribal customs are to blame for the low status of women in Muslim countries, arguing that Islamic teachings pronounce women to be inferior and subordinate to men. She also claims that reforms to give women greater rights in Muslim countries are consistently opposed by Islamic religious leaders.

As you read, consider the following questions:

1. Why are women more liberated in Turkey than in other Muslim countries, according to the author?
2. What examples from the Qur'an (Koran), Islam's Holy Book, does the author quote to support her arguments?
3. What connections does the author make between Islam, Christianity, and Judaism?

"Man enjoys the great advantage of having a god endorse the code he writes; and since man exercises a sovereign authority over women it is especially fortunate that this authority has been vested in him by the Supreme Being. For the Jews, Mohammedans and Christians among others, man is master by divine right; the fear of God will therefore repress any impulse towards revolt in the downtrodden female."

Simone de Beauvoir—The Second Sex 1949

Islam, Christianity and Judaism are patriarchal, monotheistic religions and are bound by one thing—their contempt of women!

When confronted with the issue of women's plight in Muslim countries, Muslim apologists insist that their religion has been misunderstood and that Islam actually grants women certain rights. They blame tradition and tribal societies for the low status and oppression of women.

Since Islam exerts absolute power over every aspect of Muslim society, from diet to relations between the sexes, why has it failed in fourteen centuries of its existence, to eradicate injustices against half of its adherents?

Turkey's women are the most liberated in the Muslim world. This was achieved not through Islamic reformation but through secularisation established by the founder of the modern Turkish republic Kemal Ataturk.[1] Kemal was the product of secular education and had always admired Western culture. He pursued a program of westernisation that affected all aspects of Turkish life—women were granted the vote and veiling was prohibited. If the Turkish system were to collapse and [be] replaced by an Islamic theocracy we can be certain that women's progress will be reversed and women will be at the mercy of the mullahs. In countries where there has been a [rise] in fundamentalism and reversal to strict religious law such as Pakistan, Sudan and Afghanistan women are targeted with vengeance and brutality.

Some Muslim scholars agree that Mohammed did proclaim some rights for Muslim women. For example he abolished the pre-Islamic Arabian custom of burying alive unwanted female infants. He also decreed that women could

---

1. Ataturk led Turkey from 1923 to 1938.

own and inherit property, and that women have the right to enjoy sex!

However, he did enshrine women's inequality and inferior status in immutable Quranic law accepted by Muslims as the infallible word of God.

> *Men have authority over women because God has made the one superior to the other, and because men spend their wealth to maintain them. Good women are obedient. They guard their unseen parts because God has guarded them. As for those among you who fear disobedience, admonish them and send them to beds apart and beat them.* Sura[2] 4:34

> *. . . Women shall with justice have rights similar to those exercised against them, although men have a status above women. God is mighty and wise.* Sura 2:228

Under Shari'a—Islamic law—a man can marry up to four wives. He can divorce his wife or wives by saying "I divorce you" three times. For a wife to obtain a divorce is usually very difficult. Muslim apologists claim that Muslim women have the right to divorce and that in Islam the mother is revered and respected. Upon divorce, fathers win custody of boys over the age of six and girls on the onset of puberty. Many women would be reluctant to divorce violent or polygynous husbands for fear of losing their children. Despite the exaltation of motherhood—Mohammed once told a follower that paradise is found at the feet of the mother—children are considered the property of the father with the mother being merely the caretaker. How is it possible for a Muslim man to respect his mother when immutable religious law proclaims women's inferiority and inadequacy?

Under the Shari'a, compensation for the murder of a woman is half the amount of that of a man. A woman's testimony in court is worth only half of a man's. Women are entitled to only half the inheritance of males; the reason given for these is that males have families to provide for. In sura 4:34 men are granted superiority and authority over women because they spend their wealth to maintain them; this implies that women are a burden on society and that their work

---

2. a chapter of the Qur'an (Koran)

in caring for children, household and livestock is insignificant and trivial.

Girls as young as nine can be married off by their father even if the mother disapproves of the marriage; often they end up as second or third wives of much older men. . . . Conservative clerics have resisted moves to raise the minimum age for girls. . . .

Any attempts by various governments to give women more freedoms, greater property and marriage rights have been vehemently opposed by conservative Islamists, who insist that the reforms are against Islam.

Punishing Adultery

In the Qur'an the prescribed penalty for adultery is one hundred lashes and a year in exile—sura 24:1. However, Mohammed did condemn people to be stoned to death. In one case the rabbis brought a man and a woman accused of adultery; Mohammed ordered the pair to be stoned to death. The Jews practiced stoning for adultery and it is mentioned in the Old Testament under Mosaic Law. Today many Islamic fundamentalists advocate the stoning of women and stoning does occur in many Muslim countries. . . .

In countries governed by the Shari'a a woman's testimony is worth only half of that of a man's. In Pakistan since Islamisation,[3] rape victims are charged with "zina"—sex outside marriage—and are sent to prison.

In 1977 a Saudi princess and her lover were sentenced to death and executed. The princess was separated from her husband and intended to leave the country with her lover. The execution was captured on camera by a British tourist and was televised all over the world. In Saudi Arabia women are subject to many harsh restrictions. They are forbidden to drive and most jobs are denied to them. The only evidence of their existence is the appearance of their name on their father's or husband's ID card. While women are expected to abide by a medieval and self-effacing moral code, Saudi men are importing planeloads of prostitutes from overseas and

3. Pakistan embraced Islam-based legal and government reforms when it was ruled by General Mohammed Zia-ul-Haq (1977–1988).

are buying sex-slaves from impoverished countries in addition to being permitted up to four wives.

Telnaes. © 2001 by Ann Telnaes. Reproduced by permission.

The law on adultery usually applies only to women. Since men are permitted up to four wives plus concubines they would hardly have the time for "unlawful" sex! Recently there was a case in Nigeria of a woman accused of sex outside marriage. She was sentenced to death by stoning while the man she had sex with was not charged because there was not enough evidence against him!

When Afghanistan was occupied by the Russians, women's

rights were protected by law—much to the dismay of Islamists. When the Russians withdrew Islamic fundamentalists went to work in eradicating any gains made by women. The Taliban, a product of the Madrasah—fundamentalist religious school where boys spend hours every day reciting and memorizing the Qur'an—has taken the subjugation of women to new heights. Women were barred from employment and girls [were] forbidden to attend school. Women were also denied medical care because it was illegal for women to be examined by a male doctor. Any woman caught in the company of a male not related to her was sentenced to death and women were not permitted to leave the house without being accompanied by a male relative. Some women earned a small income by baking bread; when discovered by the Taliban they were burned alive in their own ovens.

In the Indian province of Kashmir, Muslim fundamentalists have demanded that all women (even those who are not Muslim) start wearing veils. When the call was ignored Muslim thugs threw acid in the faces of uncovered women.

Female Genital Mutilation

Female genital mutilation [FGM] is an African custom that pre-dates Judaism, Christianity and Islam. It is widely practiced in African countries, the Middle East, Malaysia, Indonesia and also amongst certain ethnic groups living in Europe, North America and Australia. In Africa FGM is practiced not only by Muslims but also by some Christian and Animist groups as well.

Some Muslims believe that Islam mandates FGM and they continue its practice in order to ensure that their daughters will remain chaste until marriage. The doctrine of "chastity equals goodness" is nothing more than a device designed to control women's sexuality and to reduce women into objects "new" and "used"! Sounds familiar? In the US, Christian fundamentalists have embarked on a "chastity and family values" crusade in order to curb women's sexual freedom and autonomy.

Islam's psychotic obsession with female chastity, modesty and virginity has rendered men incapable of viewing women as equal and worthy companions. How can we expect these men to treat women decently when their religion and culture forbids it! In fact, Muslim men can relax only when their foot is firmly placed on their women's necks!

In Muslim societies religion governs all aspects of life and has priority over secular laws and local customs; therefore, the excuse that tradition alone is responsible for women's oppression is untenable. Unless Muslim apologists are prepared to back their claims by a campaign to reform their religion and improve the situation of women, their assertions that Islam is blameless in oppressing women are null and void.

Turning a Blind Eye?

There is a risk that multiculturalism and freedom of religion will ensure that tradition and religion remain eternally immutable. Should respecting other cultures mean that we should turn a blind eye to sadism, torture and brutality?

How long I wonder, will the world continue to tolerate the gender apartheid in the Islamic world and still persist in calling itself civilized?

> "The Muslim woman was given a role, duties and rights 1400 years ago that most women do not enjoy today, even in the West."

Women Are Liberated Under Islam

Mary Ali and Anjum Ali

Mary Ali and Anjum Ali are affiliated with the Institute of Islamic Information and Education, an organization that seeks to elevate the image of Islam and Muslims in North America by providing information about Islamic beliefs and history. In the following viewpoint they credit Islam's founder, the prophet Muhammad, for elevating the status of women to be equal to men. They argue that the rules found in Islam's holy writings recognize the different and complementary roles men and women play in families; while women have different responsibilities than men, their rights and obligations under Islam provide for a complete and balanced life.

As you read, consider the following questions:
1. What special rights do wives have under Islam, according to the authors?
2. What examples from the Qur'an (Koran), Islam's holy book, do the authors use to support their arguments?
3. Why do men and women have different roles and rights, according to the authors?

Today people think that women are liberated in the West and that the women's liberation movement began in the 20th century. Actually, the women's liberation movement was not begun by women but was revealed by God to a man in the seventh century by the name of Muhammad (Peace be upon him), who is known as the last Prophet of Islam. The Qur'an and the Traditions of the Prophet (*Hadith* or *Sunnah*) are the sources from which every Muslim woman derives her rights and duties.

Human Rights

Islam, fourteen centuries ago, made women equally accountable to God in glorifying and worshipping Him—setting no limits on her moral progress. Also, Islam established a woman's equality in her humanity with men. In the Qur'an, in the first verse of the chapter entitled "Women", God says,

> O mankind! Be careful of your duty toward your Lord who created you from a single soul and from it its mate and from them both have spread abroad a multitude of men and women. Be careful of your duty toward Allah in Whom you claim (your rights) of one another, and towards the wombs (that bore you). Lo! Allah has been a Watcher over you. (4:1)

Since men and women both came from the same essence, they are equal in their humanity. Women cannot be by nature evil (as some religions believe) or then men would be evil also. Similarly, neither gender can be superior because it would be a contradiction to equality.

Civil Rights

In Islam, a woman has the basic freedoms of choice and expression based on recognition of her individual personality. First, she is free to choose her religion. The Qur'an states:

> There is no compulsion in religion. Right has been made distinct from error. (2:256)

Women are encouraged in Islam to contribute their opinions and ideas. There are many traditions of the Prophet which indicate women would pose questions directly to him and offer their opinions concerning religion, economics and social matters.

A Muslim woman chooses her husband and keeps her name after marriage. A Muslim woman's testimony is valid in legal disputes. In fact, where women are more familiar, their evidence is conclusive.

Social Rights

The Prophet said, "seeking knowledge is a mandate for every Muslim (male and female)". This includes knowledge of the Qur'an and the Hadith as well as other knowledge. Men and women both have the capacity for learning and understanding. Since it is also their obligation to promote good behavior and condemn bad behavior in all spheres of life, Muslim women must acquire the appropriate education to perform this duty in accordance with their own natural talents and interests.

While bearing, raising and teaching of children, providing support to her husband, and maintenance of a home are among the first and very highly regarded roles for a woman, if she has the skills to work outside the home for the good of the community, she may do so as long as her family obligations are met.

Islam recognizes and fosters the natural differences between men and women despite their equality. Some types of work are more suitable for men and other types for women. This in no way diminishes either's efforts or benefits. God will reward both sexes equally for the value of their work, though it may not necessarily be the same activity.

Concerning motherhood, the Prophet said, "Heaven lies under the feet of mothers". This implies that the success of a society can be traced to the mothers who raised it. The first and greatest influence on a person comes from the sense of security, affection, and training received from the mother. Therefore, a woman having children must be educated and conscientious in order to be a skillful parent.

Political Rights

A right given to Muslim women by God 1400 years ago is the right to vote. On any public matter, a woman may voice her opinion and participate in politics. One example, as narrated in the Qur'an (60:12), Muhammad is told that when the believing women come to him and swear their allegiance to Islam, he must accept their oath. This established the right of women to select their leader and publicly declare so. Finally, Islam does not forbid a woman from holding important positions in government. . . .

Economic Rights

The Qur'an states:

> By the creation of the male and female; Verily, (the ends) you strive for are diverse. (92:3–4)

In these verses, God declares that He created men and women to be different, with unique roles, functions and skills. As in society, where there is a division of labor, so too in a family, each member has different responsibilities. Generally, Islam upholds that women are entrusted with the nurturing role, and men, with the guardian role. Therefore, women are given the right of financial support.

The Qur'an states:

> Men are the maintainers of women because Allah has made some of them to excel others and because they spend of their wealth (for the support of women). (4:34)

This guardianship and greater financial responsibility given to men requires that they provide women with not only monetary support but also physical protection and kind respectful treatment.

Muslim women have the privilege to earn money, the right to own property, to enter into legal contracts and to manage all of her assets in any way she pleases. She can run her own business and no one has any claim on her earnings, including her husband.

The Qur'an states:

> And in no wise covet those things in which Allah hath bestowed His gifts more freely on some of you than on others; to men is allotted what they earn, and to women, what they earn; but ask Allah of His bounty for Allah hath full knowledge of all things. (4:32)

A woman inherits from her relatives. The Qur'an states:

> For men there is a share in what parents and relatives leave, and for women there is a share of what parents and relatives leave, whether it be little or much—an ordained share. (4:7)

The status of women in Muslim countries has long been looked to as evidence of "Islam's" oppression of women in matters ranging from the freedom to dress as they please to legal rights in divorce. The true picture of women in Islam is far more complex.

The revelation of Islam raised the status of women by prohibiting female infanticide, abolishing women's status as property, establishing women's legal capacity, granting women the right to receive their own dowry, changing marriage from a proprietary to a contractual relationship, and allowing women to retain control over their property and to use their maiden name after marriage. The Quran also granted women financial maintenance from their husbands and controlled the husband's free ability to divorce.

John L. Esposito, *What Everyone Needs to Know About Islam*, 2002.

Rights of a Wife

The Qur'an states:

> And among His signs is that He created for you mates from among yourselves that you may live in tranquility with them, and He has put love and mercy between you; Verily, in that are signs for people who reflect. (30:21)

Marriage is therefore not just a physical or emotional necessity but, in fact, a sign from God! It is a relationship of mutual rights and obligations based on divine guidance. God created men and women with complementary natures and, in the Qur'an, He laid out a system of laws to support harmonious interaction between the sexes.

> . . .They are your garments and you are their garments. (2:187)

Clothing provides physical protection and covers the beauty and faults of the body. Likewise, a spouse is viewed this way. Each protects the other and hides the faults and complements the characteristics of the spouse. To foster the love and security that comes with marriage, Muslim wives have various rights. The first of the wife's rights is to receive *mahr*, a gift from the husband, which is part of the marriage contract and required for the legality of the marriage.

The second right of a wife is maintenance. Despite any wealth she may have, her husband is obligated to provide her with food, shelter and clothing. He is not forced, however, to spend beyond his capability and his wife is not entitled to make unreasonable demands. The Qur'an states

> Let the man of means spend according to his means, and the man whose resources are restricted, let him spend according to what Allah has given him. Allah puts no burden on any person beyond what He has given him. (65:7)

God tells us men are guardians over women and are afforded the leadership in the family. His responsibility for obeying God extends to guiding his family to obey God at all times.

A wife's rights also extend beyond material needs. She has the right to kind treatment. The Prophet said,

> The most perfect believers are the best in conduct. And the best of you are those who are the best to their wives.

God tells us He created mates and put love, mercy and tranquility between them.

Both men and women have a need for companionship and sexual needs and marriage is designed to fulfill those needs. For one spouse to deny this satisfaction to the other, the temptation exists to seek it elsewhere.

Duties of a Wife

With rights come responsibilities. Therefore, wives have certain obligations to their husbands. The Qur'an states:

> The good women in the absence of their husbands guard their rights as Allah has enjoined upon them to be guarded. (4:34)

A wife is to keep her husband's secrets and protect their marital privacy. Issues of intimacy of faults of his that would dishonor him, are not to be shared by the wife, just as he is expected to guard her honor.

A wife must also guard her husband's property. She must safeguard his home and possessions, to the best of her ability, from theft or damage. She should manage the household affairs wisely so as to prevent loss or waste. She should not allow anyone to enter the house whom her husband dislikes nor incur any expenses of which her husband disapproves.

A Muslim woman must cooperate and coordinate with her husband. There cannot, however, be cooperation with a man who is disobedient to God. She should not fulfill his requests if he wants her to do something unlawful. A husband also should not take advantage of his wife, but be considerate of her needs and happiness.

A Balance in Society

The Qur'an states:

> And it becomes not a believing man or a believing woman, when Allah and His Messenger, Muhammad, have decided on an affair (for them), that they should (after that) claim any say in their affair; and whoso is rebellious to Allah and His Messenger, he verily goes astray in error manifest. (33:36)

The Muslim woman was given a role, duties and rights 1400 years ago that most women do not enjoy today, even in the West. These are from God and are designed to keep balance in society; what may seem unjust or missing in one place is compensated for or explained in another place. Islam is a complete way of life.

| "*The emergence of political Islam and the coming to power of Islamic regimes in the Middle East . . . has unleashed [a] wave of state sponsored terrorism against women.*"

Islam Condones Honor Killings

Azam Kamguian

Each year hundreds—possibly thousands—of women are killed by their relatives to preserve family "honor." Women are killed for a wide variety of perceived immoral offenses, including marital infidelity, "allowing" oneself to be raped, seeking a divorce, or even failing to serve a meal on time. Many of these killings, which often go unreported and unpunished, occur in Muslim nations and in Muslim communities in Western nations. In the following viewpoint Azam Kamguian argues that honor killing is in part a reflection of Islamic laws and values. She claims that those who perpetuate honor killings often use Islamic concepts and passages from Islam's sacred writings to justify the practice. Kamguian is a writer whose works include *Islam, Women, Challenges and Perspectives.* She is the chairperson for the Committee to Defend Women's Rights in the Middle East, an independent, nongovernmental organization aiming at educating the public, raising awareness, and campaigning for women's rights in the Middle East.

As you read, consider the following questions:

1. Why do available statistics on honor killings underestimate the practice, according to Kamguian?
2. What Islamic concepts and teachings contribute to the problem of honor killing, according to the author?

Azam Kamguian, "The Lethal Combination of Tribalism, Islam & Cultural Relativism," www.secularislam.org, August 27, 2003. Copyright © 2003 by the Institute for the Secularization of Islamic Society. Reproduced by permission of the publisher and the author.

Hundreds of women get shot, burned, strangled, stoned, poisoned, beheaded or stabbed every year in Muslim inhabited countries because their male relatives believe their actions have soiled the family name. They die so that family honour may be preserved. According to tribal and religious culture a woman is a man's possession and a reflection of his honour. It is the man's honour that gets tarnished if a woman is 'loose'. Being killed deliberately and brutally is, in fact, a price that victims pay for attempting to practice their minimal human rights.

It takes far less than a pre or extramarital relationship for a woman to be condemned as dishonourable and deserving of death. There is no 'typical' case one can speak of: 'honour crimes' can include a husband killing his wife for leaving the house too often, a son killing his mother to prevent her from remarrying, a brother killing his sister and her husband for marrying without the family's consent, a man killing his wife for refusing to wear the veil when leaving home. Reputation and rumour play an active role in instigating honour crimes and the killing of women. This phenomenon is comparable to the emphasis on the chastity of wives in Victorian morality. Because the concepts of male honour and female subservience are deeply ingrained in Islam and in tribal culture, honour killings have become commonplace in Arab and Middle Eastern countries, in other Muslim inhabited countries and Muslim immigrant communities in the West.

The available statistics in honour killings show just the tip of an iceberg. The reality is far darker. The statistics do not show the number of female suicides provoked, or engineered to cover up an honour killing, nor the number of mysterious disappearances. Many honour killings never get reported or registered. Many are mislabeled.

In Egypt between 1998–2001 suspicion of 'indecent' behavior was the reason behind 79 per cent of all crimes of honour. The women were killed just because of rumours or suspicions that they may have crossed the line. The UN statistics for 1997 show: Yemen 400, Pakistan over 1000, Egypt 52, and Jordan 25–35. The UN also reported that as many as 5000 women and girls worldwide were killed last year by family members, a majority of them for the 'dishonour'.

Tribal Dimension

According to tribal culture and values, women's 'misbehavior' is not only a shame on the family but on the community, the village, the tribe, the neighbourhood and the neighbours. The tribe and community participate in the killing by endorsing it. If and when the family fails to kill the woman, the tribe will cast it out. During the pre-Islamic period Arab society was patrilineal and Bedouin, where the highest authority was the father or male members of the family. At the time slavery was rife and women were perceived to be the property of their family or tribe with the potential of bringing disgrace to their kinsmen. The Bedouins before Islam practiced female infanticide. Later, the Islamic religion attempted to regulate sexual relationships and transgressions: prostitution, zina, infanticide were prohibited, and sex out of wedlock and adultery were brutally penalised. Yet, the pre-Islamic code of conduct survived, creating a powerful value system, parallel to Islam and practically and mutually nurturing and supporting one another. . . .

Islamic Dimension

According to Islamic culture and tradition, girls are taught from early childhood about "eib", which means shame, and "sharaf", which means honour. Everywhere, girls are reminded that their most important mission in life is to remain virgin until they marry. Boys are also taught to have "ghayrat", meaning to be zealots. All these concepts are Islamic, and that is why the killers always defend their acts of murder by these concepts. According to the UN statistics, the majority of these murders occur in Muslim inhabited countries and Muslim immigrant communities in the West. In [a] majority of cases, the murderers and their defenders refer to this verse of the Koran that allows husbands to beat their wives:

> *As to those women on whose part ye fear disloyalty and ill-conduct, admonish them, refuse to share their beds, beat them.* Koran, chapter 4, verse 34.

There are numerous similar verses in the holy book, which promote and prescribe violence against women. Laws regarding honour killing provide that men accused of these killings are not to be prosecuted for murder but for 'crimes of honour'. And the law is usually on the man's side, not only in the Middle Eastern and the Central Asian countries, but shamefully, in Western countries too. They often let murderers go unpunished or let them off with a light sentence.

Islam and Honor Killings

Each year hundreds of Muslim women die in "honor killings"—murders by husbands or male relatives of women suspected of disobedience, usually a sexual indiscretion or marriage against the family's wishes. Typically, the killers are punished lightly, if at all. In Jordan a man who slays his wife or a close relative after catching her in the act of adultery is exempt from punishment. If the situation only suggests illicit sex, he gets a reduced sentence. The Jordanian royal family has made the rare move of condemning honor killings, but the government, fearful of offending conservatives, has not put its weight behind a proposal to repeal laws that grant leniency for killers. Jordan's Islamic Action Front, a powerful political party, has issued a fatwa, or religious ruling, saying the proposal would "destroy our Islamic, social and family values by stripping men of their humanity when they surprise their wives or female relatives committing adultery."

Honor killings are an example of a practice that is commonly associated with Islam but actually has broader roots. It is based in medieval tribal culture, in which a family's authority, and ultimately its survival, was tightly linked to its honor. Arab Christians have been known to carry out honor killings. However, Muslim perpetrators often claim their crimes are justified by harsh Islamic penalties, including death for adultery. And so religious and cultural customs become confused.

Time, December 3, 2001.

Religious discourse is misogynist and has an important role in enforcing the double standards that society and the laws apply to women. A man remains honourable even if he has sexual relations with three-quarters of earth's women, but this is not the case for a woman's voluntary sexual relationship.

Islamic Shari'a law is strict in the matter of adultery. According to Islamic law, [the] penalty for adultery for unmarried women (and men) is 80 lashes and stoning for married women (and men). Islam and the Shari'a law have kept and try to keep the monopoly over the killing of women in the matter of adultery. When unable, however, Islamists wholeheartedly support honour killings and exonerate the murderers. Theoretically, Islam does not sanction honour killing yet the majority of Islamic leaders and Imams wholeheartedly promote and support it.

Tribal and political Islamic groups are against less harsh punishments for honour crimes arguing that this would set women on the road to promiscuity. According to a Jordanian Islamic lawmaker, *"Women adulterers cause a great threat to our society because they are the main reason that such acts take place."* Political Islamic groups and Islamic leaders basically reject abolishing of or any changes to the laws regarding honour killings, arguing that it would lead to the moral disintegration of society and will get rid of major social deterrents to relationships between men and women. Islamic leaders consider any changes to these laws as a violation of the Shari'a that would encourage adultery, and as an attempt to legalise obscenity.

In the Region

The emergence of political Islam and the coming to power of Islamic regimes in the Middle East in the last two decades has unleashed [a] wave of state sponsored terrorism against women. Countries such as Iran, Algeria, Morocco, Afghanistan, Pakistan and the Sudan further constrained the lives of women by introducing more and more aspects of the Shari'a into their legal systems. A century of struggle for the separation of state from religion came under constant attack, being seen by Islamists as a conspiracy against Islam and the East. Women were the first targets. In this context, the most brutal violence against women, including mandatory veiling, a complete system of sexual apartheid, stoning and honour killing, were and are all in rise.

This continues while members of younger generations especially girls, become better educated and more exposed to the world outside. Increasingly, they are rebelling against parents and families who cling to traditions that prohibit socialising with the opposite sex, choosing a husband for themselves, or visiting freely with friends outside the home. The rising social pressures on both generations have led to an alarming increase in honour killings, beating and other violence within families as well as suicide among urban and rural girls and women.

As far as the legal system [is] concerned, neither the Shari'a law, family laws based on the Shari'a or civil states laws are systematically or consistently applied to women by most Arab countries. The legal process is selective, with the worse possible elements being in its treatment of women. . . .

In the West

Though honour killing may not seem so surprising in countries such as Jordan, Saudi Arabia and Yemen, that it exists in the heart of Europe in the 21st Century is indeed both shocking and shameful. But sadly, this is where the reactionary idea of Cultural Relativism is used to justify women's victimization and to excuse Islam and backward traditions.

In many of the sizable Muslim immigrant communities in Europe, brutality against women is justified in the name of respecting 'other's' culture and religion. How can we respect any culture or religion that endorses violence and terrorism against women? Over the past twenty years cultural relativism has led to a culture of tolerating intolerance. Criticising these unacceptable traditions, cultures and religious beliefs and practices has been labeled racism and Islamophobia. Human beings are worthy of respect but not all beliefs can or should be respected. It is perfectly feasible to love the believer but hate the belief. Relativism and respect for misogynism is no shield against racism. Quite the opposite. It promotes racism by depriving women and girls living in European and Middle Eastern countries of their universal rights and civil liberties.

While murderers have repeatedly and openly defended their acts by referring to Islam and the Koran in justification, many feminists, the mainstream media and western intellectuals largely try to explain these murders as part of the prevalent patterns of domestic violence against women in western societies. While the murderers, whether in the Middle Eastern countries or within the Muslim communities in the West, openly state that their acts of murder are "crimes of honour", and that they are merely following the directions set down in their religious beliefs, the apologetic 'western' intellectuals repeatedly assure us that it is not Islam and backward traditions that are to blame, but that these murders are part and parcel of the common pattern of violence that is happening to western women too.

Equally worrying is the tendency among political leaders, academics and feminists, to reject the application of human rights discourse to personal matters, describing human rights as a purely western concept foisted on the more traditional societies of the east without adequate debate.

And as far as European governments are concerned, there shouldn't be different bases for people's rights in European countries. All should be considered as citizens and equal before the law. Society is duty bound to safeguard and protect the rights of women and girls from Muslim origin. This could be done only by abolishing all the respective discriminatory laws and regulations against these girls and women. This could be done only when there is no respect, excuse and legal justification for the misogynist Islamic and traditional beliefs and practices. . . .

What Is to Be Done?

A society ruled by misogynist tribal and Islamic laws and values permits the killing of women. Honour killing is a reflection of ancient patriarchy embracing Islamic misogyny and ancient tribal values. In the West, in collaboration with cultural relativism, it has created a deadly mix that has brutally victimised many young girls and women.

Honour killing, which contradicts many basic human rights and values, is clearly connected to the subordination of women. The prevailing culture of discrimination and misogyny in Islamic religion and society will not change without implementing comprehensive and radical sociopolitical and legal changes in the situation of women.

The civil rights of Arab citizens generally depend on their status, class, tribal affiliation and proximity to the regimes. This altogether discriminatory culture strongly affects women. It is not easy to dislodge let alone eliminate honour killing and other forms of violence in the absence of a radical transformation of the unequal social and economic order.

The only effective strategy to abolish honour killings is to safeguard and advance women's rights and status; by fighting against Islamic, patriarchal and tribal traditions; by separating religion from the state; and by forming secular and egalitarian governments in the region. Then, when equality before the law, civil rights, human rights, justice, freedom are achieved and safeguarded for all citizens regardless of their gender, class or race, women will benefit by extension. The struggle against honour killing is inseparable from the struggle for women's civil liberties, for the separation of Islam from the State, the struggle against political Islam and Islamic States in the region. All restrictive and backward cultural and moral codes and customs that hinder and restrict women's freedom and independence as equal citizens must be abolished. Severe penalties must be imposed for the abuse, intimidation, restriction of freedom, degradation and violent treatment of women and girls.

These are the tasks of women's liberation movement along with the progressive and egalitarian movements in the region as well as in the West.

4

"The abuse and killing of women for alleged honor crimes is not Islamic."

Islam Does Not Condone Honor Killings

Samana Siddiqui

In the viewpoint that follows, Samana Siddiqui, a Muslim and daughter of Pakistani immigrants, examines the issue of honor killing—the practice of killing women for behavior that is believed to dishonor their family. Writing in response to a series of television documentaries about honor killings in Pakistan and Jordan, she argues that honor killing is a cultural practice that is not condoned by the Islamic religion—a fact she believes many Western reports and documentaries gloss over. Such media reports thus create and inflame prejudice against Islam and Muslims, she believes. The fact that honor killings do occur in some Islamic countries does not mean that the honor killing is an Islamic practice, she argues, any more than the fact that domestic violence occurs in the United States means that American culture inherently supports the battering of women. Siddiqui is a staff writer for Sound Vision, an Islamic multimedia company based in Chicago, Illinois.

As you read, consider the following questions:
1. Why is Siddiqui dissatisfied with Western television documentaries about honor killings in Jordan and Pakistan?
2. What is the common response to media coverage of honor killings, according to the author?
3. How prevalent is the problem of domestic violence in the United States, according to Siddiqui?

The images were horrific.

A Muslim Pakistani woman's disfigured hands, raised in supplication, were displayed for audiences to see. This was her punishment for "dishonoring" her family.

A young man in Jordan described how he recited the Quran as he strangled his sister to death. Her crime: "dishonoring" the family.

Both of the scenes, the former from a BBC television documentary, the latter from one broadcast on the Canadian Broadcasting Corporation (CBC), were part of a spring 1999 media focus on the practice of "honor killings". It is interesting to note that both documentaries aired the same week, along with one on the ABC television network in the United States.

"Honor killings" are extreme crimes of passion. When a woman is suspected of having sex outside of marriage, her husband, father, brother or other male relatives kill her.

Does the practice of honor killings in Muslim countries like Pakistan and Jordan confirm that Muslims are cruel and barbaric towards women? Does it prove that Islam allows injustice against half of humanity?

No, it does not.

Culture, Not Religion

The documentaries themselves made an interesting distinction. Both noted that honor killings are a cultural practice, not a religious one. In the CBC's, it was even mentioned that honor killings are practiced among Jews and Christians of the region.

Yet, the overall impression is that honor killing is condoned by the teachings of Islam.

While journalists included disclaimers (i.e. that honor killings are cultural, not Islamic), they buttressed their pieces with shots of veiled women, mosques, as well as people praying and reciting the Quran. That makes it hard to believe the practice isn't Islamic.

The result is continuing confusion and misunderstanding about Islam and Muslims. Muslim Americans are still accused of following a faith that treats half of humanity oppressively. Muslim women are pitied. Muslim men are reviled. Both elicit disgust. After all, who would choose to follow a religion that allegedly treats women in such a barbaric fashion?

The disgust can express itself in more than just attitudes. Misunderstanding Islam has led to death threats against Muslims, vandalism against their homes and mosques, as well as physical assaults.

What Does Islamic Law Say About Honor Killings?

Under Islamic law (Shariah), sex outside of marriage is a capital crime both men and women are to be punished for. However, two things are critical to remember. First, the burden of proof is extremely stringent: four witnesses must have seen the actual act of intercourse between those accused. Second, following due process of law, the punishment can only be administered by an Islamic government. There is no room for vigilante justice.

In addition, under Islamic law, those who take justice into their own hands would themselves be punished. In the case of honor killings, they would be tried for murder.

Honor killings, therefore, have no place in Islam.

Most Muslim countries, including those that claim to rule according to the Shariah prosecute crimes according to decades old colonial laws that incorporate tribal and social customs. The result is that in many cases, the "law of the land" does not reflect the ethos and worldview of the ruled. This partly explains vigilante justice, as well as the culture of lawlessness that has developed in many of these countries.

Today, with growing awareness about the crime of honor killing, more people in places like Pakistan are speaking out. Thanks to the hard work of women's and Muslim activists, honor killings receive more publicity. As a result, the government now uses its terrorism laws to punish these crimes of passion.

In his 1987 book *Television Culture*, John Fiske notes that in general, Third World countries are only mentioned in the news when something tragic or conflictual takes place. They are presented as places of natural disasters, famine, social revolution and of political corruption. Those events are considered the rule, rather than the exception. The coverage of

A Problem of Pre-Islamic Culture

What is commonly paraded in the Muslim world as "Islam" is sometimes only the pre-Islamic ignorance and culture that enabled men to justify the burying of girls alive. The Qur'an not only prohibits the action of physically burying them alive, but also dispels the myths that demonize and vilify the female gender so that burying girls alive seems a reasonable thing to do. The people of Arabia buried them because they believed that women are promiscuous and that this promiscuity would bring shame to the family. This practice was prohibited during the lifetime of the Prophet (saw), yet killing women was later resumed by the Arabs as "honor killing." Today in "honor killings", physical abuse and psychological torture we also see other forms of "killing" women in more subtle, culturally accepted and 'legal' ways. The objective in every case is to prevent society from being affected by the feminine qualities of womanhood, cast as evil by Arabs in much the same way and perhaps for the same reasons as the Christians and Jews blamed women for the sin of Adam, thereby condemning us to a history of shame and humiliation as punishment for the sin that Allah ta'ala forgave. The Qur'an informs us that both Adam and his companion disobeyed Allah, and that both shared the penalty and the mercy of Allah, through which they both found forgiveness. Despite this, Arab societies and many that have been "Arabicized" have perpetuated the ignorance and womanhatred of pre-Islamic Arabia by various means, including the denial of women's right to share in the establishment and development of Islamic society.

Anisa Abd el Fattah, *Crescent International*, June 16–30, 2001.

honor killings as well as similar crimes around the world seem to fit this pattern. There is little discussion of the underlying causes of the problem.

Honor Killings in America

Honor killings are ugly. So are the crimes against women committed regularly in the United States.

According to the National Organization of Women, every day four women die in this country as a result of domestic violence. That's approximately 1,400 women a year, according to the FBI.

Also consider the following statistics from the US Department of Justice:

- Every 9 seconds, a woman is battered
- In 1992, the US Surgeon General ranked abuse by husbands and partners as the leading cause of injury to women aged 15–44
- Up to 50 percent of all homeless women and children in the United States are fleeing domestic violence
- There are nearly three times as many animal shelters in the United States as there are shelters for battered women

Given these facts, would anyone argue or even allude that Christianity, the religion of 83 percent of Americans, is responsible for the oppression of women?

Of course not.

A history of abuse and violence in families, socioeconomic factors, and jealousy on the part of husbands and boyfriends are just some of the explanations given for the abuse of women, especially wives and girlfriends in America. Jealousy is the main component of sex-related murder cases in the Third World, as well.

Walk into a women's shelter that is not targeted to a specific ethnic or cultural group, and you will find women of all races, colors, and religions.

The abuse and killing of women for alleged honor crimes is not Islamic. Nor is the abuse of women inherently as "American as apple pie".

Muslims and non-Muslims must work together to end the ongoing oppression of women in their societies. However, this cannot be done by fueling stereotypes through biased and one-sided reporting. It must be done with properly contextualized information and understanding of each other.

Periodical Bibliography

The following articles have been selected to supplement the diverse views presented in this chapter.

Haleh Afshar	"Women in Islam: The Western Experience," *Middle East Journal*, Autumn 2002.
Zainah Anwar	"Ending the Patriarchy: To Claim Their Rights, Muslim Women Cannot Leave It to Men to Define Islam," *Time*, March 10, 2003.
Christopher Dickey and Marie Valla	"Sexism in the *Cités*," *Newsweek*, August 18, 2003.
James Emery	"Reputation Is Everything—Honor Killings and Islam," *World & I*, May 2003.
Yotam Feldner	"'Honor' Murders—Why the Perps Get Off Easy," *Middle East Quarterly*, December 2000.
Delinda C. Hanley	"Saudi Arabian Women Dispel Myths and Stereotypes," *Washington Report on Middle East Affairs*, May 2001.
Riffat Hassan	"Women in Islam: Body, Mind, and Spirit," *Christian Social Action*, May/June 2000.
Hillary Mayell	"Thousands of Women Killed for Family 'Honor,'" *National Geographic News*, February 12, 2002.
Katha Pollitt	"As Miss World Turns," *Nation*, December 23, 2002.
Beena Sarwar	"Women Pay as Fundamentalism Grips Pakistan," *Ms.*, April/May 1999.
Jane I. Smith	"Women in Islam (Clothes and Convictions)," *Christian Century*, January 30, 2002.
Madhavi Sunder	"Piercing the Veil," *Yale Law Journal*, April 2003.
Time	"The Women of Islam: The Taliban Perfected Subjugation. But Nowhere in the Muslim World Are Women Treated as Equals," December 3, 2001.
Nayereh Tohidi	"'Islamic Feminism': Perils and Promises," *Middle East Women's Studies Review*, Fall 2001.
Amina Wadud	"A'ishah's Legacy," *New Internationalist*, May 2002.
Bronwyn Winter	"Fundamental Misunderstandings: Issues in Feminist Approaches to Islamism," *Journal of Women's History*, Spring 2001.

CHAPTER 4

How Will Islam's Future Be Shaped?

Chapter Preface

Many Muslims look toward the long history of Islam to find clues about its future. For most of the history of Islam, Muslims have customarily divided the world into two parts: *Dar al-Islam* and *Dar al-Harb*. The literal meaning of *Dar al-Islam* is "House of Islam"; it is also sometimes translated as "House of Peace." It refers to the regions and nations of the world governed by Islamic law. The literal meaning of *Dar al-Harb* is "House of War," and refers to parts of the world not subject to Islamic law.

Much of Islam's history is the story of how Muslims have sought to expand the House of Peace—an expansion often carried out by military conquest. Historian Karen Armstrong notes that expansionism was justified by "Muslim jurists" who "taught that, because there was only one God, the whole world should be united in one polity and it was the duty of all Muslims to engage in a continued struggle to make the world accept the divine principles and create a just society." For these reasons, she writes, the House of War "should be made to surrender to God's rule." Historian Paul Fregosi asserts that a basic goal of Muslims today continues to be "to expand and extend Islam until the whole world is under Muslim rule."

In the first decades of its existence, in the 600s and 700s, Islam quickly spread through much of the known civilized world, reaching west to Spain and east to India. Over the next millennium, *Dar al-Islam* grew to encompass several (sometimes rival) empires that comprised most of the Middle East and northern Africa, as well as parts of Asia and Europe. However, by the early twentieth century, most of Europe and parts of Asia had been reclaimed by non-Islamic powers, most of the Islamic dynasties themselves had fallen, and much of the Islamic world in the Middle East, Africa, and Asia was under the control of Great Britain, France, and other Western colonial powers. The nation-states that emerged when the Western colonial empires broke up later in the twentieth century were often led by Western-educated elites who shunned Islamic law and modeled their governments and economics on secular and Western ideas.

In addition, refugee movements, immigration, as well as individual conversions to Islam have resulted in millions of the world's Muslims residing in countries such as the United States with no tradition of Muslim rule or Islamic law.

These developments have left present-day Muslims with various ideas about what can be done to strengthen Islam's role in the world. While many agree that expanding *Dar al-Islam* is still a fundamental Islamic duty, differences exist in how to accomplish it. For some, the primary imperative is to restore Islamic law in the governments of Muslim-majority countries and to increase the political and economic influence of Muslim nations. Other Muslims seek a retreat from nationalism and call for the political unity of all Muslims regardless of country. Yet others stress the need to spread the message of Islam and to seek expansion of the faith by convincing nonbelievers to convert to Islam. The viewpoints in this chapter provide a sampling of opinions on the future of Islam and how that course will affect the House of Peace and the House of War.

1

| *"Muslims need to reassert in a modern context the fundamental truths of the Koran . . . based on broad principles of justice and equality."*

The Muslim World Should Modernize by Adopting Some Western Values

Abdullahi Ahmed An-Na'im

Abdullahi Ahmed An-Na'im is a professor of law at Emory University in Atlanta, Georgia; his books include *Toward an Islamic Reformation: Civil Liberties, Human Rights, and International Law.* In the 1980s, when he was on the law faculty at the University of Khartoum in the Sudan, he was a member of an Islamic reformist group and was held briefly as a political prisoner. In the following viewpoint he argues that Muslims need to place the basic teachings of Islam into a modern context in order to adapt Islam to today's world. He rejects both Western cultural domination and radical Islamic fundamentalism, including demands by fundamentalists to make the sharia (the historic law code of Islam) the starting point of establishing an Islamic state. Values, such as women's equality, that developed in the West should be recognized as universal and be incorporated within Islam, he concludes.

As you read, consider the following questions:

1. Why is An-Na'im opposed to the implementation of the sharia?
2. What distinction does An-Na'im make between the Mecca and Medina messages?

Abdullahi Ahmed An-Na'im, "The Islamic Counter-Reformation," *New Perspectives Quarterly*, vol. 19, Winter 2002. Copyright © 2002 by Blackwell Publishers, Ltd. Reproduced by permission.

The tragedy of Islam today is that the Muslim leadership has locked itself into being intimidated by its extremist elements. These Muslim leaders, whose moral bankruptcy and weakness are represented by the opulent lifestyles of the Saudi Sheikhs, live on the fringes of Islam as well as Western civilization. They lack the essence of either. In that sense, they are twice as corrupt and twice as Satanic as radical Muslims claim the West to be.

As a result, a few militant and highly motivated gangsters— real criminals—are holding Muslim cultures and Muslim leadership hostage.

The primary motivation of radical Muslims is a reaction to Western neocolonialism and, more significantly, Western cultural domination. The revolt against Western cultural domination is legitimate, but how that revolt develops is the key question for Islam today.

The complete and immediate implementation of Shari'a (the historic code of Islam), which is what radical Muslims such as the Taliban demanded, is the least Islamic position for a Muslim to adopt today. To try to build a new Islamic identity in this way is tantamount to saying that Islam stands for repression and discrimination at home and aggressive war abroad.

In order to sustain and strengthen the Islamic faith, Muslims need to reassert in a modern context the fundamental truths of the Koran and the Prophet's original Mecca message which was based on broad principles of justice and equality. Only by removing the serious inconsistencies between their historical Islamic self-identity and the realities of the modern world can Muslims effectively challenge Western domination. If they fail, they will lose their Islamic identity and tradition altogether.

Counter-Reformation Before Reform

The benefits of Western secularism for the Muslim world, such as technology, human rights and civil international relations, are only superficially entrenched. In the Iranian revolution [1979], these frail acquisitions of civilization were swept away wholesale because they were not indigenous or legitimized from within Islam itself.

The Islamic world never experienced the Enlightenment or had its own Reformation out of which the Islamic equivalent of Western concepts of democracy, human rights and civil liberties could have developed. The emergence of a bourgeoisie and heightened individual consciousness which presaged these great European movements did not arise in the Muslim context until the present day.

Today, Islam is in a period of pre-Reformation. Paradoxically, the coming Islamic Reformation has its roots in the Muslim reaction to the muted influences of European modernity.

In the 19th century, Muslims thought they could reap the benefits of the European Enlightenment by emulating it—such as in Turkey and Egypt with the adoption of the European codes. Elitist Muslims saw that they could neutralize the rising expectations of the masses in this way. This has continued up to the present time.

Today, because advanced communications and transportation enable Muslims to travel, read and watch television, they readily see that their institutions and doctrines are extremely inadequate in terms of even superficially emulating the West. However, this surface modernization has raised the economic expectations and heightened the political frustration of Muslims because of the lack of freedoms at home.

At the same time it has made Muslims feel that they have lost touch with their own Islamic identity and tradition. Especially in the wake of decolonization, they understand that national self-determination must be of an Islamic nature. Caught in a kind of limbo between tradition and modernity, Muslims have found themselves where their leaders have taken them—superficially Islamic and superficially modern.

One attempt to resolve this dilemma has been the great Islamic "counter-reformation." This reaction against Western influence and the search for an historical Islamic identity is precisely why the Reformation will ultimately come about. The historical model promoted by Iran has remained an ideal which Muslims sentimentalize and glorify, believing that it can miraculously overcome all their problems. When it is seen to fail, a new Islamic identity that accommodates human rights and international law will come about. In this sense, our counter-Reformation is the prelude to the Islamic Reformation.

Meanwhile, the situation grows worse. There may be a great deal of killing and human suffering before things get better. Fundamentalism is growing. We have been visited with the experiences of Iran, Pakistan, the Sudan and Afghanistan. Egypt remains a target. It is extremely significant because it is the most vital and vigorous center of learning in the whole Muslim world. If Egypt should fall, many other Muslim countries would fall very quickly. Khomeini[1] types or Sunni fundamentalists like the Muslim Brothers, who are also in Syria and Tunisia, are likely to succeed unless Muslims can develop progressive reforms that are Islamically genuine.

However, it is an optimistic and religiously determined path we are taking. We believe all this human suffering has been visited upon us to excite our religious imagination, to sharpen our intellect and our moral response. It has prepared us for the next step—realization that Islamic self-identity based on Shari'a is an historically dated identity that needs to be reformed.

Shari'a and Human Rights

Shari'a is the law of Islam developed by early jurists from basic sources: the Koran, which Muslims believe to be the final and literal word of God, and the living example of the Prophet Himself. Shari'a is very broad and comprehensive. It includes worship rituals—how to pray, cleanliness for worship, how to fast and rules for social etiquette—how to dress and how to wash. There is no inconsistency with these rituals and questions of human rights.

What is a problem with Shari'a is that part which has to do with penal law, rights and civil liberties and the treatment of minorities, non-Muslims and women. It is these aspects of the Islamic code that have tended to hit the Western headlines—the quick-justice amputations for theft or veils on women.

For political expediency, some Muslim governments emphasize the penal aspects as window dressing to publicize

1. Ayatollah Khomeini was a fundamentalist Shiite Muslim cleric who led the 1979 Islamic Revolution in Iran.

their commitment to Shari'a without genuinely being committed to other, more important rules about economic and social justice and legitimate political power. For example, if there were a genuine commitment to Shari'a in Saudi Arabia, the hereditary monarchy would be rejected as illegitimate because, according to Shari'a, the personal lifestyle and conduct of the ruler are alone the basis for his claim to rule.

Unfortunately, because they are afraid of creating the conditions for civil strife, many Islamic jurists have been co-opted by the regimes in power and have contributed to the distortion of Islam.

The Contribution of the West

The first Islamic state was established in Arabia, around 622, in the city of Medina after the Prophet Mohammed's migration from Mecca. It is only in the last 100 years that the historical model of Shari'a, based on the circumstances of Medina, has lost its legitimacy and moral validity. The notion of aggressive jihad [holy war] has become morally untenable as a means of conducting international relations; and the rise of the modern human rights movement has tumbled the moral foundations of segregation and discrimination against women and non-Muslims.

Human rights and the international rule of law were contributions to civilization from the West. Since the West has had a very significant role in developing the totality of the human experience, Muslims are entitled, even required, to take advantage of these positive achievements.

In each cycle of the growth of civilization, a new contribution is added to the total course of human experience. The ancient Romans incorporated what the Greeks had contributed. Roman civilization was, in turn, developed and promoted by Muslims. Then Muslims handed it back to Europe. The Islamic task now is to reconcile human progress with traditions; to reject the remnants of colonial domination and spiritual corruption, of whatever source, while accepting the standards of economic and political justice and the rights of individuals.

For example, as Muslims, we should accept female equality. That is a universal value. But the way we develop our indigenous response to this challenge is our business. Mahmoud Mohammed Taha, the leader of the Republican Brothers in the Sudan who was executed by President [Gaafar] Numiery, was first imprisoned for challenging the colonial authorities who had arrested a woman for circumcising her daughter. Although Taha opposed the practice of circumcision as a means of subordinating women, he felt that such an unhealthy and oppressive practice should be countered by indigenous medical and moral education, not by the imposition of European norms by colonial authorities.

As Muslims, we should also accept the full human dignity of non-Muslims and their right to be equal citizens. The very ideas of the national state, constitutional government, limitations of power and equality regardless of sex or religion are part of the universal values to which Islamic law must adapt.

Not a Static Faith

Islam cannot survive as a static faith, buried in history. It was always meant to be a dynamic worldview, adjusting to change. In reality, the shariah is nothing more than a set of principles, a framework of values that provide Muslim societies with guidance. But these sets of principles and values are not givens; they are vigorously derived from within changing contexts. As such, the shariah is a problem-solving methodology rather than law. It requires individual believers and societies to exert themselves and to reinterpret the Koran and the life of the Prophet Muhammad.

Ziauddin Sardar, *New Statesman*, February 17, 2003.

However, regarding penal law, I cannot find a way, in principle, to abolish what is perceived to be the harshest aspects of the law—amputations and floggings. But we can deemphasize their importance as primary instruments of justice while we place the highest priority on social and economic justice.

Penal law should not be applied in the spirit of vengeance and intimidation. For example, in the Jewish tradition there is still a wide range of about 50 offenses punishable by death, but Jewish jurists have developed pre-requirements and procedural safeguards that effectively preclude application of penalties. Human judgment cannot abolish the offense because it is a matter of religious principle, but human judgment can decide whether the conditions for enforcement of the penalty have been satisfied.

Superfundamentalist Reform

In considering the reform of Islam, it is useful to think in terms of the combined roles played by Thomas Aquinas and Martin Luther in the adaptation of Christian tradition to the development of the modern world. This analogy illustrates both the commitment to tradition and fundamental religious notions, while at the same time seeking reformation and a challenge to orthodoxy.

In Mecca, for the 13 years before His migration to Medina, the Prophet received the first part of the Koran—the Mecca part. This Mecca period established the moral and ethical foundation of the Muslim community.

Because this peaceful and voluntary Mecca message of fundamental social and economic egalitarianism was violently rejected in Mecca and Arabia in general, the Mecca message was not suitable for that stage of human development. Thus, the Prophet's migration to Medina not only signified a tactical move to seek a more receptive environment, but also a shift in the content of the message itself.

The rest of the Koran—the Medina message—which later became codified in Shari'a as the model for an Islamic state by the majority of Muslims, was a step backward. For example, there are many verses in the Koran from the Mecca message which say there is no compulsion in matters of religion or belief and people should be left to decide for themselves whether they want to believe or not believe. In the Medina message, there are verses that say one should go out and fight infidels wherever one finds them and kill them. There are verses which say one should fight Christian and Jewish believers, making them submit to Muslim rule or be subjugated by force.

Now, according to Islamic belief, each message, including Judaism and Christianity, is valid only to the extent that it is relevant and applicable to changing people's lives. So, it was very necessary, logical and valid in that context for the Prophet to apply the Medina message. But the Medina message is not the fundamental, universal, eternal message of Islam. That founding message is from Mecca.

So, the reformation of Islam must be based on a return to the Mecca message. In order to reconcile the Mecca and Medina messages into a single system, Muslim jurists have said that some of the Medina verses have abrogated the corresponding earlier verses from Mecca. Although the abrogation did take place, and it was logical and valid jurisprudence at one time, it was a postponement, not a permanent abrogation. If we accept the process as a permanent abrogation, we will have lost the best part of our religion—the most humane and the most universal, egalitarian aspects.

The Mecca verses should now be made the basis of the law and the Medina verses should be abrogated. This counter-abrogation will result in the total conciliation between Islamic law and the modern development of human rights and civil liberties. In this sense we reformers are superfundamentalists.

The key to our reformation will be a positive and receptive attitude toward the totality of the human experience. What we find to be consistent with our fundamental principles, we accept, whatever the source.

For example, the democratic component of Western experience, not the capitalistic component, is a positive aspect. The social component of the Marxist experience, not the atheist or totalitarian aspect, is a positive aspect. We would not accept the humanism of the Western Enlightenment unqualified. We accept that God is the Creator in the first place; Man the creator only in the second place—to the extent that he is a reflection of the original Creator. For this reason, the Islamic religious orientation would remain even in a neutral state that retains a functional separation between state and religion.

If universal values are not adapted from within indigenous traditions, reform only foments the very cultural reaction witnessed in the Islamic world today.

"We [Muslims] must not make the mistake of accepting the present state of the world in general, and the West in particular."

The Muslim World Should Reject Western Values and Embrace Traditional Islam

Muzaffar Iqbal

Muzaffar Iqbal is the founder and president of the Center for Science and Islam and editor of its *Journal of Islamic Perspectives on Science*. In the following viewpoint he argues that much of the Muslim world has suffered under European rule, which has undermined Islamic beliefs and traditions. He argues that many people who call for the "reform" of Islam have blindly embraced Western values and have neglected Islam's proper role as a political force and shaper of society. The billion people that constitute the global Muslim community (*ummah*) must resist the decay of both Western and Islamic civilization and embrace Islam not only as personal belief but as a total way of life and superior alternative to Western civilization.

As you read, consider the following questions:
1. What "fruits" of the West's scientific and industrial revolutions mesmerized Muslims who traveled to Europe, according to Iqbal?
2. Why does the author believe docility to be the antithesis of Islam?
3. What does Iqbal see as weaknesses in Western civilization?

Muzaffar Iqbal, "The Prophet's Seerah and the Contemporary State of the Ummah," www.muslimedia.com, October 1, 2003. Copyright © 2003 by *Crescent International*. Reproduced by permission.

The celebration of the life of the Prophet of Islam (*saw*) is being held when almost the entire Muslim world is under neo-colonial rule. This is perhaps the darkest time of our history, when truth and falsehood have become indistinguishable for most, and the forces of kufr [unbelief] have penetrated deep into the Muslim world.

This terrible state of affairs has not emerged overnight; it is the result of a long process. In order to understand our situation and seek guidance, we must examine the processes that have brought us to our present predicament. But before that we need to understand the condition of the Ummah [Muslim community] today. What is meant by neo-colonialism? How does it operate? Who are the people using this new method to subjugate the Ummah, and what does it mean to be governed by proxy rulers?

European Colonialism and Islamic "Reform"

After the collapse of Muslim rule in Ottoman Turkey, Mughal India and Safavid Iran, almost the entire Muslim world was occupied physically by European powers. During the occupation they established new institutions in almost all spheres of collective life. These institutions were used to cultivate a new generation who looked like us but behaved like them. In the century of colonial rule, steps were taken to undermine the Islamic tradition. This aspect of colonization was the destruction of a tradition, a way of life and a unique orientation of society toward the Creator. This barbaric policy has received little attention; in fact, this willful destruction of a civilization has been called "bringing modern education, industry, science and technology" to the Muslim world; many Muslims see this aspect of colonization as the colonizers portray it. Most nineteenth-century reformers also saw it so.

They considered British and French education far superior to their own. Many travelled to England and France, witnessed the "fruits" of the scientific and industrial revolutions, and came back mesmerized. They saw technological inventions and called them miracles. They were so impressed by the wide and clean roads, by the water-supply systems and the town-planning of their rulers, that they were ashamed to belong to a community that they learnt to regard as riddled with illiteracy, poverty and disease, in towns and villages where there was nothing "civilized" by their new standards.

Thus a terrible verdict was passed on Islamic civilization, not only by the colonizers but also by the colonized: people whose standards had been changed; people for whom the material wealth and glamour of Western civilization had become the only definition of advancement and progress. True, there were many ills in Muslim societies, especially enormous problems concerned with the development of infrastructure and institutions suitable to a changing world. But these problems were misunderstood and exaggerated; a general verdict was passed that the whole of Islamic civilization was backward, ill-suited for changed times, and in need of reform.

The reformers' discourse was, in fact, a product of the new "educated elite" that had emerged in the colonized lands. This elite considered Western civilization the most advanced and sophisticated civilization, and all others as backward and primitive. When applied to Islamic civilization, this verdict discredited everything achieved during the previous millennium in the sciences, architecture, education and health-systems. It could not, however, reject Islam outright. So it made allowance for faith by creating a deep fissure in the Islamic tradition. This operation separated personal faith from all other aspects of Islam, thus producing a generation that possessed a dormant faith and lived a life shaped by Western ideals.

Trivializing Islam

This schizophrenia showed in their blindly imitating the colonizers' ways. Thus there emerged thousands of educational institutions, teaching a curriculum in which Islam either was absent or had been abstracted from real life by a reductive process that made the Qur'an a book wrapped in cloth and kept on a shelf so high that it was out of reach, even physically. Likewise the Prophet (*saw*) was made into a sacrosanct being whose memory was celebrated year after year but whose life had no relation to the lives of those who revered him.

This abstraction of Islam, this caricature of a faith, pro-

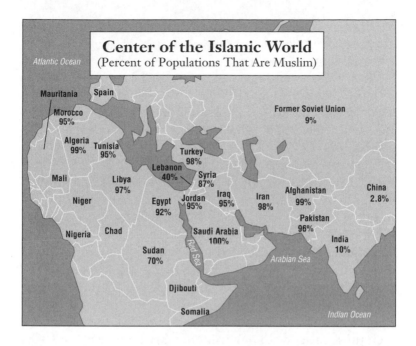

duced a society in which Islam had lost its role as the shaper
of the social order. Once Islam was reduced to theoretical
formulations, Muslim society lost its inheritance that had
been cultivated for over a millennium. One of the worst
parts of this loss was accomplished by a master-stroke: the
forces of occupation simply discarded the Islamic languages
and substituted their own, thus making a vast amount of
spiritual, ethical and intellectual guidance inaccessible to future generations of Muslims.

Robbed of their languages that had linked them to centuries of scholarship, wisdom and literature, the Muslims
were uprooted from the very soil that could have helped
them to recover from the occupation. Herein lie the roots of
our present condition. It is in this process of intellectual and
emotional genocide that we find clues to changes that are
now apparent all over the Muslim world.

Imagine an occupying army in Washington DC announcing that English is no longer the language in which the business of the state will be conducted. This would not only render thousands of skilled administrators redundant, it will
also subvert four hundred years of historical process by mak-

ing thousands of scholars, scientists, teachers and thinkers illiterate. It must create a new generation of administrators, scholars, writers, teachers and institutions that align themselves with not only the newly-imposed language but also with the civilization and lifestyle of the occupying force. And if this occupation were to last a hundred years, it would create a truly new order. This is exactly what happened in the Muslim world.

During the nineteenth century this new order manifested itself through educational and administrative institutions that are still operative in almost all Muslim lands. But despite the violence with which this new order was enforced, Islam could not be uprooted completely. Reduced to *'ibadah* [devotional observances] and made abstract and unreal, still it remained in the hearts of millions. They had lost the tradition of learning that once produced profound thinkers, scholars and scientists, but their faith could not be destroyed completely. We see this even in the most Westernized lives: even those raised with only rudimentary knowledge of Islam wish to get married and be buried according to traditional Islamic practices.

Despite all the social, political and economic forces against it, Islam remained the faith of the vast majority, and continued to guide the religious life of society, although its social, political and economic aspects were overshadowed. Thus there emerged a severance between the various components that comprise Islam, producing a schizophrenic society which was being pulled in opposite directions. This severance is still the dominant feature of the Ummah today; it is no exaggeration to say that it is the Ummah's worst sickness.

This severance separates faith (*iman*) from deeds (*a'mal*), education from knowledge and insight, personal conduct from social conduct, politics from ethics, and beliefs from practices. It permeates all Muslim societies. It is to be found in all classes of these societies, at all levels.

A Religion of Strength

Thus an Ummah of more than a billion has become impotent, ineffective and oppressed. It is inconceivable that Islam has produced a social body without goals and purpose, consisting of weak and ineffective individuals who have no collective direction, goal or purpose. Islam by definition is a dynamic and effective system with a definite goal and direction, which exists as the result of a covenant (*mithaq*) between the Creator and His creation: a covenant that pulsates with strength and creativity. It also produces coherence in individuals and societies by guiding individual and collective lives.

Thus severance and dissonance are un-Islamic characteristics: docility and weakness are not the result of Islam, as some claim, but the antithesis of Islam. The life of Allah's Messenger (*saw*) proves this. His is the best-recorded life in human history, and not a single report suggests a docile, ineffective and split state. On the contrary, his whole life is characterized by a decisiveness that knows no hesitation. Whether in danger of defeat and death at Uhud, or at his triumphant entry into Makkah, we see him in a resolute faith that knows no doubt. His was a life governed by the inner radiance and strength that comes from total obedience to and acquiescence in the will and command of Allah.

The social and political order that came into existence in Madinah, and spread to a large part of the world within fifty years of his death, also shows the signs of great inner coherence and outward decisiveness. This resolution, this clarity of means and ends, this unity of inner certainty and outer action, were passed on to the Companions (*ra*). Whether we examine the small battalion of Muslims that arrived in Samarqand to establish an Islamic order in Central Asia, or the Muslims who went to the ancient seats of learning in Alexandria, we find the same unity, the same steadiness, the same confidence in the truth and beauty of Islam.

Islam is not a faith that comes into existence on Fridays; it is a way of doing and a mode of being. It cannot be patched with any foreign philosophy or way of life. It is impossible to think of a Muslim being a Muslim in a *masjid* [mosque] and not a Muslim in the office or laboratory or home. This coherence is one of the most fundamental aspects of Islam. During colonization this inner coherence of the Ummah was destroyed. It is this destruction that has produced a split in the Islamic polity today. As a result of this split the Ummah has been reduced to an ineffectual mass of undirected lives.

Many diagnoses and prescriptions have been made of our present state. This forlorn state has been described by thinkers in diverse ways during the last century. Some have suggested that the calamity is a result of our departure from the Qur'an and Sunnah [sayings of Muhammad]; others have said that it is the result of falling behind Europe in science and technology; still others blame it on this or that social, economic or political factor. Perhaps all these diagnoses have some degree of truth. What it is important that we achieve, however, is a general acceptance that there is something terribly wrong with the followers of Islam; that our docile existence is in contradiction to our faith, which by definition is a faith of action, strength and resolution.

The Decay of Civilizations

This verdict needs no evidence: the sheer force of reality verifies it; the present state of the Muslim world is indeed one of defeat. But I wish to qualify this verdict. The decay and decadence, the fall of ethical action, the economic and political subjugation and the military weakness of the Muslim world, all are indeed undeniable, but we must not make the mistake of accepting the present state of the world in general, and the West in particular, as an enviable alternative. The fact is that all civilizations have decayed, and Western civilization most of all, by Qur'anic standards. This distinction is important because otherwise we are liable to fall into the trap of self-laceration, glorification of *taghut* [false gods], and total confusion. Let there be no doubt about the nature of decay. The decay of the West is of the worst kind: the very criteria of right and wrong have been lost. The very basis of existence as a social entity has been eroded during the last fifty years. This must be kept in mind, because when a civilization reaches such a state, though it may still have material wealth and military power, it is bound to collapse eventually. History testifies amply to this general rule; there is no reason to believe that Western civilization will be an exception.

"We should work vigorously on the borders of the Islamic world, in those cultures where the fundamentalists have not yet been able to destroy all hope of a better future."

The United States Must Contain Radical Islam

Ralph Peters

In the following viewpoint Ralph Peters argues that the future of Islam lies not within the oil-rich Arab states where Islam began, but in non-Arab countries in Asia and Africa that contain half the world's Muslims. It is in such places as Turkey, Pakistan, India, and Indonesia, he argues, that an ongoing struggle exists between the fanatical and fundamentalist version of Islam promulgated by the Arab world and a more progressive and tolerant version of the faith. The United States, Peters argues, should actively encourage the development of respect for law and human rights in those nations. In addition, he contends that America should work to "roll back" militant Islam in places where it is threatening to expand. Peters, a retired American military officer, is a columnist and author of *Beyond Terror: Strategy in a Changing World.*

As you read, consider the following questions:
1. Why have past U.S. diplomatic efforts in the Islamic world been counterproductive, according to Peters?
2. What actions of Saudi Arabia does the author find threatening?
3. What observations does Peters make about Islam in Indonesia?

In the heyday of the Cold War, when the world made grisly sense, strategists touted a rollback policy toward communism. In the event, we rolled back precious little and had to be content with holding the line, at least until 1989. But "rollback" was a strategy decades ahead of its time. . . . It is an eminently sensible approach to radical Islam.

Wrong Players

Our efforts in the Islamic world have been largely wasted, when not counterproductive. We have spent half a century backing the wrong players. Oil smeared our vision and we concentrated on the self-destructive Arab states and oil-rich Iran, where our policy . . . [was] built upon hollow assets and self-delusion. After Israel, listless Egypt remains the leading recipient of our aid dollars, while we have enmeshed ourselves in Middle Eastern confrontations we do not understand and cannot solve—but which excite venomous hatreds toward us as a reward for our efforts. We insist that Saudi Arabia, a police state that funds Islamic extremism around the world, is our friend. Our president plays host to its de facto king at his ranch. And we are pledged to protect those bazaars of terror, the Gulf states, with our blood.

But the Arab world, rich and poor, is nearly hopeless. With a few, strategically unimportant exceptions, it has given itself over to the narcotic effects of hatred and blame. Arab civilization cannot compete on a single productive front in the 21st century. And there is nothing we can do about it. If the Arab world will not repair itself, no amount of indulgence will make a difference. We have wasted decades on governments and populations who need us as an enemy to justify their profound failures.

When well-meaning officials, academics or pop singers assure us that Islam is not the problem, they are utterly wrong. Islam, as promoted by Saudi Arabia and practiced by fanatics elsewhere in the Arab world, is precisely the problem. The Saudi variant attempts to buy off the forces of history at home, while exporting the Middle Ages to countries as diverse as Indonesia, Afghanistan and Turkey. The purpose of Saudi proselytizing seems to be to re-create in every Muslim culture the limited prospects of the Arab world.

A Mighty Struggle

At present, there is a mighty struggle underway on Islam's frontiers for that religion's soul. Those frontiers should be the focus of our efforts to encourage Islam's humane tendencies. As useful as military engagement may be in places such as Georgia and the Philippines—along Islam's geographic frontiers—constructive engagement on Islam's social, economic and spiritual frontiers would be even more helpful in the long term. The military addresses today's problems; tomorrow's challenges are already fermenting.

Plenty of hope remains for non-Arab, Muslim-majority states to reward their citizens with progress and tolerance. Instead of wasting further efforts on the Middle East, where the military remains our optimal tool, we should work vigorously on the borders of the Islamic world, in those cultures where the fundamentalists have not yet been able to destroy all hope of a better future, and where Islam is still a developing faith, not merely a tomb for the living.

Thus far, we haven't even gotten the numbers right. Arab populations are a minority within Islam, but their regressive form of religion has been poisoning one non-Arab state after another with an infusion of petrodollars, dogma and anti-Western vitriol.

Three non-Arab countries, Indonesia, India and Pakistan, contain nearly half the world's Muslims. Add those of Central Asia, Turkey, the Philippines, Malaysia, Kosovo, Bosnia, Azerbaijan and that struggling, vilified democracy, Iran, and the Arab states begin to look as over-valued as they are recalcitrant. Even Nigeria is more promising in the long term than Egypt. If we want to roll back the inhumane variants of Islam and to promote constructive cooperation and the emergence of rule-of-law, market-driven states, then we should turn our energies to the lands of possibility, rather than wasting further efforts on Arab states utterly opposed to reform.

A Different Approach Needed

The process will require diligence, as well as a more sophisticated understanding of foreign cultures than we currently possess. The brusque, do-it-or-else American approach will not work. Countries need to be nudged, watched, encouraged, rewarded and trained—and, when they deserve it, punished intelligently, rather than clumsily. In states such as Indonesia, from which I recently returned more hopeful than I was before my journey, the situation demands continuing acupuncture, not a single dose of heroic surgery. Our policy must be comprehensive, yet each state's case must be handled according to its own fears and eccentricities.

Consider, briefly, those three most populous "Muslim" states—India (which has more Muslims than Pakistan), Pakistan and Indonesia. In India, where chronic interfaith violence obscures larger successes, the best thing we can do to defuse radical tendencies is to build a healthier, mutually respectful relationship between the world's two most creative democracies. In Pakistan, where each political party vied with the others to excel in corruption and duplicity, the situation is far more difficult. Only the military has any chance of rescuing Pakistan from the blame-game fundamentalism all previous political leaders encouraged for selfish ends. Frankly, there may be more hope for Afghanistan, which has hit bottom and may climb back up. But even in Pakistan, the price of engagement is small, while the cost of walking away is enormous.

Look to Indonesia

With the exception of Iran, which is struggling to become a progressive, rule-of-law democracy, Indonesia is the least understood Muslim state. While its population of over 200 million is almost 90% Islamic on paper, less than 20% would qualify as good Muslims by Saudi standards. No other country offers so wide a variety of Islamic practices as does Indonesia, where Hinduism and Buddhism prevailed far longer than Islam has yet done. Folk beliefs still haunt the mosques and Muslim schools, and "pure" Muslims struggle, with only marginal success, to persuade the others that the local, Sufi-influenced forms of Islam are all wrong. Jakarta, not Jeddah, is where the future of Islam will be decided. And we are not even seriously engaged, although our extremist enemies have been pouring in money and peddling hatred for decades.

The Islamic world is rich in possibilities and remarkably

162

various. By betting on the Arab states, we have been letting our best prospects slip away—abandoning global Islam to the apostles of terror. In military terms, we have "left the battlefield to our enemies." If we really believe that Islam is a great world religion, we need to treat it as such and engage it where it is still developing—on its vibrant frontiers, not in its arthritic Arab homelands.

"For [the Muslim world] to be trapped in [radical Islamism] is to travel back in time to the dark ages."

Muslims Must Defeat Radical Islam

Ayaz Amir

Ayaz Amir is a columnist for *Dawn*, a Pakistani newspaper. The following viewpoint, taken from a January 2003 column, describes the state of the Muslim world in the context of America's war against terrorism. Amir argues that America and the West feel threatened by Osama bin Laden, leader of the terrorist group al-Qaeda, which was responsible for the terrorist attacks of September 11, 2001. But he goes on to assert that bin Laden and his ideas pose a greater threat to the Muslim world than they do to the West. Bin Laden, Amir argues, is a leading representative of the view that Muslims must return to ideals of Islam's past. Such views trap the Muslim world in intolerance and backwardness, Amir contends. The defeat of Islamic fundamentalism as represented by bin Laden and his followers, he concludes, is ultimately the responsibility not of America but of Muslims themselves.

As you read, consider the following questions:

1. How have political elites failed in Muslim nations, according to Amir?
2. What agreements and disagreements does the author express with America's war on terrorism?
3. Why has the West maintained superiority over the Muslim world, in Amir's opinion?

W e like to think—or rather we comfort ourselves with the thought—that the West, especially the United States, is caught in a frenzy of Muslim-bashing. We try not to realize that our own condition, a mixture of ineptitude and backwardness, is an invitation to bashing. We are not the victims of a cosmic conspiracy. We are responsible for our backwardness ourselves.

We have not managed our affairs well. This is true of almost all the countries that call themselves Islamic. Even when the end of colonialism came, the world of Islam continued to be exploited—again not because of any malevolent conspiracy but because the bankruptcy of ideas that lay at its heart invited exploitation.

Challenges of the Modern World

Israel dominates its Arab neighbours not simply because of American dollars and American arms. If it was simply a question of money, Arab petrodollars could push Israel into the sea. Israeli domination comes from the power of knowledge and technology. Compared to its neighbours it is a developed country. For its own kind, if not for the Palestinians, it is also a democracy. Both these things give it a commanding edge. Which does not whitewash its repression in the occupied territories. But that is hardly what I am saying.

Our answer to the challenges of the modern world has been twofold. The affluent classes of the Muslim world, including its rulers, have been happy to become appendages or clients of the West. The disadvantaged or those at the bottom of the heap have discovered comfort and security in a crude form of Islamism.

If our elites have failed their respective people, if we have been left behind in the race of knowledge and ideas, our excuse is not that we have been poor learners or that we have a long way to go before we catch up with the West. We like to say that we have been bad Muslims and have not kept faith with the true tenets of Islam.

So towards a self-defined purity of Islam many of us have tried to return in the conviction that this journey back in time holds the key to all our problems.

This journey into the past took no cruder form than the

emergence of the Taliban.[1] It has taken no cruder form than the ideas firing the zeal of Osama bin Laden and his followers.[2] The West feels threatened by Al Qaeda terrorism. But perhaps we may consider that Bin Ladenism is a greater threat to the world of Islam than it is to the West.

For the West it is but a physical threat in the form of terrorism. For the world of Islam it is a threat more grave and sinister; for it to be trapped in Bin Ladenism is to travel back in time to the dark ages of Muslim obscurantism. It means to be stuck in the mire which has held the Islamic world back.

Since therefore this threat for us is less military and more spiritual or intellectual, we have to be careful about the choice of weapon. The black-and-white simplicities of the Bush administration won't do for us because our concerns and requirements are different. The demonization of Iraq fits in with American preconceptions not ours. . . .

The threat to the Muslim world comes from other things. From authoritarianism, from the fact that apart from the half-exceptions (please note, half-exceptions) of Turkey, Malaysia and Pakistan, the concept of democracy is alien to the Muslim world. The threat to it comes from intolerance and the lack of knowledge.

Bin Ladenism is the purest distillation of these problems. We shouldn't require Washington to tell us that it is in our interests to exorcise this evil. We should have the sense to realize this on our own. But at the same time this fight should be ours and we should be defining its agenda and setting out its aims.

America's War on Terrorism

This is not what is happening. The Bush administration is doing all the defining while lesser states are being pressed into active service in America's 'war on terrorism' and its impending war on Iraq[3] (both things having got mixed up somewhere down the line).

1. The Taliban was a strict Islamic regime that ruled most of Afghanistan from 1996 to 2001.   2. Osama bin Laden, who was raised in Saudi Arabia, is the leader of al-Qaeda, an Islamic terrorist network responsible for several terrorist incidents, including the September 11, 2001, attacks.   3. The United States invaded Iraq in March 2003.

Far from improving matters, this war on terrorism is making things worse for the Islamic world. For it is feeding resentment against the West—and by extension, the values it stands for: secularism, tolerance and democracy—and at the same time making heroes and martyrs of those recruited to the standards of Bin Ladenism. Across the Muslim world as the West is demonized for launching a 'war of civilizations' against Islam, popular sentiment veers towards those shadowy figures and organizations seen standing up to the new imperialism.

The Duty of American Muslims

American Muslims have generally been more critical of injustices committed by the American government than of injustices committed by Muslims. This has to change.

For the last few years, I have been speaking publicly in Muslim forums against the injustice of the Taliban [regime in Afghanistan prior to 2001]. This criticism of a self-styled Muslim regime has not always been well-received. Some Muslims have felt that public criticism of the Taliban harms Muslim solidarity. Others have questioned my motives, suggesting that I am more interested in serving a feminist agenda than an Islamic one. My answer to the apologists has always been—who has the greatest duty to stop the oppression of Muslims committed by other Muslims in the name of Islam? The answer, obviously, is Muslims.

I have not previously spoken [prior to September 11, 2001] about suicide attacks committed by Muslims in the name of Islam. I did not avoid the subject—it simply did not cross my mind as a priority among the many issues I felt needed to be addressed. This was a gross oversight. I should have asked myself, Who has the greatest duty to stop violence committed by Muslims against innocent non-Muslims in the name of Islam? The answer, obviously, is Muslims.

Ingrid Mattson, Beliefnet.com.

In other words, Bin Ladenism is seen not as something primitive but as a movement symbolizing the spirit of resistance. In other words, the sources of terrorism strengthened even as its manifestations are assailed.

Pity the Islamic world whose kings, emirs and dictators are once again policemen in a crusade not of their choosing. During the cold war the same Muslim regimes (except for Egypt), now foot soldiers in [George W.] Bush's war on terrorism, were in the forward trenches of the US's war against communism. None more so than Pakistan which has never felt more secure than when labelled as America's most allied ally.

There is nothing wrong in being America's friend except that between that and a client who is rewarded only so long as he does his patron's dirty work (and is then discarded), there's a world of difference.

But who are we to educate the West? We can plead and in some cases expostulate. But we are in no position to convert the West. But why should we even be thinking on those lines? Our problem is to convert ourselves. We have to convert our thinking and remove the shackles of obscurantism from our minds if we are to know the meaning and value of freedom and dignity.

National dignity and sovereignty are empty phrases as long as minds are enslaved and our only wisdom is borrowed wisdom. We have to pull down the walls of authoritarianism and make our political systems more democratic if at all we want to improve our lot and gain some respect among nations.

The Flame of Knowledge

The flame of knowledge is one and indivisible. Down the ages it has passed from civilization to civilization. When it was with the Egyptians, the Mesopotamians and the Chinese, theirs were the civilizations which shone the brightest. When it passed to the Greeks they were the world's leaders in science and philosophy.

For a thousand years Rome was the centre of the world. Hindu mathematicians used modern numerals when the rest of the world was unaware of them. When the shadows lengthened over the Byzantine Empire, the torch of learning, one and indivisible since the beginning of time, passed to the Islamic world where it remained for several centuries. When the Islamic world fell into decline, this same torch passed to the West where it has remained since the 15th century.

The West is superior to us because the eternal flame of knowledge and learning is in its keeping. And as long as this holds true, not all the oil in the world can deliver the Muslim world from its backwardness. To the extent that countries like Japan and China have altered their destinies, they have done so by warming themselves at the same flame.

We must remember that of all hierarchies in the world, that of knowledge alone knows no caste or creed. It is not Christian or Muslim or pagan but simply knowledge and those wanting a place in the sun must look into no other mirror but this flame for their salvation.

"Progressive Muslims in America are taking their inspiration from Islamic scholars trained in Western universities who tend to be critical of authoritarian interpretations of Islam."

American Muslims Seek to Americanize the Islamic Faith

Ahmed Nassef

Somewhere between 4 and 8 million Muslims reside in the United States—a number that is rapidly growing. In the viewpoint that follows, Ahmed Nassef argues that a gulf exists between American mosques and other religious institutions, which tend to be very conservative, and the liberal views of many Muslim American men and women. He argues that Islam may well evolve in the United States to better reflect prevalent American values regarding women's equality, tolerance, and other matters. Nassef, a writer and marketing consultant, is the founder of MuslimWakeUp.com, an online magazine.

As you read, consider the following questions:
1. Where have many Islamic clergy had their training, according to Nassef?
2. What barriers to participation in religious life do American Muslim women face, according to the author?
3. What evidence of a progressive movement within American Islam does Nassef describe?

Ahmed Nassef, "Tailor Muslim Practices to Fit Life in America," *Christian Science Monitor*, www.csmonitor.com, August 4, 2003. Copyright © 2003 by The Christian Science Publishing Society. Reproduced by permission of the publisher and the author.

O mid Safi wanted to go the extra mile to make sure his children experienced an Islamic environment. So he and his family made the one-hour drive to their nearest Islamic Center in Syracuse, N.Y., every week, and he enrolled his son in Sunday school there.

Only men were allowed to use the grand main entrance to the mosque. "Women have to use a back entrance right next to the trash dumpster and go down to the basement," Mr. Safi remembers. "It felt fake for me to go through the front door and for my wife to have to use the back entrance. After a while, I could not justify to my conscience continuing to go and sending my children there."

Safi, assistant professor of Islamic studies at Colgate University and author of "Progressive Muslims," stopped attending the mosque, and now counts his family and a small group of students as his spiritual community. His experience is not unique among Muslims in the United States—a population estimated at more than 6 million and often cited as the fastest growing religious group in the country.

A Gulf Between Muslim Americans and Islamic Institutions

This gulf between the highly conservative nature of most Muslim American institutions and the liberal views of many Muslims born and raised in America is reflected in issues such as the role of women and literalist readings of religious texts. It has sown the seeds for a progressive Muslim movement that is reinterpreting much of what the faith means and how it is reflected in daily life.

What Muslim Americans are going through is no different from the experiences of other faith communities that preceded them here. The success of the Conservative and Reform movements in the US as alternatives to Orthodox Judaism, for example, has transformed the meaning of the faith for millions of Jewish Americans.

Similarly, the increasing number of native-born Americans who are adopting the faith (constituting about one-third of the total Muslim American population) and Muslim Americans from recent immigrant backgrounds—so many of whom are far removed from their parents' and grandparents' immigrant experiences, with their particular cultural interpretations of Islam—are looking for an Islam that reflects their lives in America.

Increasingly, this is translating into a disengagement from existing Muslim institutions in the US and a search for alternate communities.

An American Style of Islam

Many American Muslims privately feel that many Middle Eastern Muslims have so infused their faith with anti-Americanism, tolerance of terrorism, or other customs (like subjugation of women), that it is polluting Islam.

Even before [the September 11, 2001, terrorist attacks], American Muslims were growing their own style of Islam (just as Christians, Jews, Buddhists, and Hindus did when they immigrated). The new form is deeply rooted in the Qur'an, but features a more prominent role for women, an emphasis on democracy, and less hostility to the United States. This evolution has been happening here in part because many Muslims are now second generation and because about a third of U.S. Muslims are African-American with no particular allegiance to the Middle East.

Steven Waldman, Beliefnet.com.

Practically all American mosques are led by people who have no academic training in Islam, or who have received their training from overseas Islamic academies. Most of these have been taken over by highly conservative elements aligned with the extremely conservative Wahhabi interpretation of Islam championed and funded by the Saudi Arabian monarchy. But progressive Muslims in America are taking their inspiration from Islamic scholars trained in Western universities who tend to be critical of authoritarian interpretations of Islam and who treat the real diversity of Muslim societies more inclusively.

Today, American mosques and advocacy groups, whose representatives are most commonly called on by the media to speak for Muslim Americans, reflect only a fraction of the larger Muslim American community.

A study on US mosques conducted in 2000 by four of the main Muslim American national organizations showed that 2 million of the estimated 6 million Muslim Americans attend Muslim religious institutions at least once or twice each year, and of those, just 411,060 attend mosques regularly. Even allowing for possible exaggeration and duplication—because the survey relied on mosque representatives for its information—the results still raise issues that most Muslim American organizations are afraid to tackle. The most obvious one is that two-thirds of Muslim Americans don't publicly participate even in the most minimal cultural manifestations of their faith (like a Roman Catholic who celebrates only Christmas Mass or a Jew who attends synagogue only during the High Holy Days).

In fact, America's traditional Muslim institutions are isolated from the daily reality of life in America.

Excluding Women

For one thing, they continue to systematically exclude women from participation. Not only do practically all US mosques shut women out of the top leadership position, fully half of them either officially forbid women from serving on their governing boards or, in cases where there is no such specific prohibition, women have not served on these boards over the past five years.

Women who do attend mosques and who aren't willing to fulfill traditional roles find it hard to participate actively. For Farah Nousheen, a young Muslim American filmmaker who just completed "Nazrah," a documentary on Muslim American women, her alienation reached such a level that, after searching through mosques in the Chicago and Seattle areas and finding the same stifling atmosphere, she decided to stop attending altogether. "My experience had a lot to do with being a woman in an environment where almost all the leadership were men. At prayers, women sat in a separate area with all the crying kids. It made me feel less important," says Ms. Nousheen, "There are a lot of people out there who feel like they don't belong."

Far from moving toward inclusiveness in the way they deal with women, mosques seem to be doing the opposite. Today, fully two-thirds of mosques force women to pray in a separate room from men or behind a curtain, compared to slightly more than half in 1994. Given this development, it is no surprise that women represent only 15 percent of attendees at the weekly congregational prayers.

Another element that is driving progressive Muslims away from traditional mosques is the preoccupation with literalism and the imposition of foreign customs on a faith that prides itself on its universalism. Sermons delivered by nonnative English-speakers on esoteric topics, such as the intricacies of ablution and the ritual washing before prayers, are the rule—not the exception.

For people like Katelin Mason, a young American Muslim convert and a graduate student of Islamic studies, the identification with Islam by the traditional Muslim American leadership of specifically cultural expressions, such as wearing particular clothing, is a distortion of the faith. "Wearing hijab [head covering] and having a beard have taken priority," she wrote in a recent article for our online magazine, MuslimWakeUp.com. "When the focus is on appearance, actions and intent become less important. When appearance loses importance, piety emerges."

But much of the media is all too ready to accommodate the stereotypes of what Muslim Americans look like. As Omid Safi points out, "Whenever these groups have been called on to appear in the media, it is usually through a middle-aged bearded man with an accent. We rarely see African-Americans, or women not in full hijab, and this certainly is not what our community looks like. Not all Muslim American men have beards, and many Muslim American women don't wear the full hijab."

A New Movement

But there are signs that a grass-roots progressive Muslim movement is finally taking hold.

Over the Internet, progressive Muslim mailing lists and websites are becoming increasingly popular. Groups like the Progressive Muslim Network and the Network of Progressive Muslims engage in discussions—on everything from matters of ritual to social relationships—that would be unheard of in neighborhood mosques. The online magazine MuslimWakeUp.com which I cofounded, has featured articles that are openly critical of conservative interpretations of Islam—and according to the web-ranking company Alexa, it has become the highest-ranked website geared to Muslim Americans in just six months of operation.

A slew of books on progressive Islam in the past few years has energized many Muslim Americans to begin organizing their own conferences and gatherings. In April [2003], a group in Washington, D.C. organized the first Progressive Islam conference, where women and men prayed side by side, and women had the opportunity to lead prayers.

Sufism, the Islamic mystical trend that emphasizes spirituality over legalism and is exemplified by the popular poetry of Rumi, represents another haven for progressives.

"The only places I have felt comfortable have been Sufi congregations, because they are generally more tolerant and inclusive. They keep the focus on the values and principles of Islam as a living inspiration. They are imbued with the highest values and are not focused on the particulars of law and cultural manifestations," says Amina Wadud, Islamic studies professor at Virginia Commonwealth University and author of "Qur'an and Woman."

As with any great world faith, Islam has been very open to transformation, as illustrated by its rich sectarian history—a centuries-old genre of work exists in Islamic literature that is devoted to the study of various Muslim theological, mystical, and philosophical movements. And unless traditional Muslim American institutions and leaders are willing to deal with reality, more and more Muslims will feel compelled to find alternatives that address their spiritual concerns.

This could very well mean the formation of a new school of thought, with its own mosques and institutions, that is faithful to the universal principles of Islam.

That could only be a positive step for Americans of all faiths, especially if the result is an Islam that is inclusive, tolerant, less authoritarian, and more reflective of Muslims in America.

*"The Muslim population in this country
... includes within it a substantial body
of people ... who share ... a hatred of
the United States."*

American Muslims Seek to Islamize American Society

Daniel Pipes

Daniel Pipes is the author of numerous books and articles on Islam and the Middle East, including *Militant Islam Reaches America*. In his writings Pipes makes a distinction between the traditional religion of Islam and Islamic fundamentalism (or "Islamism"), which Pipes describes as a totalitarian political ideology that rejects all Western influences and embraces a strict adherence to sharia (Islam's holy laws). The following viewpoint was first published shortly after the September 11, 2001, terrorist attacks, at a time when many Americans, including President George W. Bush, were affirming the patriotism of American Muslims. Pipes argues that Muslims differ from other religious groups in that a substantial minority of Muslims in America are Islamists who seek to transform the United States into a Muslim nation. Pipes concludes that Americans must be wary of efforts by Muslims to undermine American customs, including its traditional separation of government and religion.

As you read, consider the following questions:

1. What fault does Pipes find with statements by President George W. Bush and other leaders?
2. Why is assuming control over America so important to some Muslims, according to the author?

Daniel Pipes, "The Danger Within: Militant Islam in America," *Commentary*, November 2001. Copyright © 2001 by *Commentary*. Reproduced by permission of the publisher and the author.

I n the aftermath of the violence on September 11,[1] American politicians from George W. Bush on down have tripped over themselves to affirm that the vast majority of Muslims living in the United States are just ordinary people. Here is how the President put it during a visit to a mosque on September 17: "America counts millions of Muslims among our citizens, and Muslims make an incredibly valuable contribution to our country. Muslims are doctors, lawyers, law professors, members of the military, entrepreneurs, shopkeepers, moms and dads." Two days later, he added that "there are millions of good Americans who practice the Muslim faith who love their country as much as I love the country, who salute the flag as strongly as I salute the flag."

These soothing words, echoed and amplified by many columnists and editorial writers, were obviously appropriate at a moment of high national tension and amid reports of mounting bias against Muslims living in the United States. And it is certainly true that the number of militant Islamic operatives with plans to carry out terrorist attacks on the United States is statistically tiny. But the situation is more complex than the President would have it.

The Muslim population in this country is not like any other group, for it includes within it a substantial body of people—many times more numerous than the agents of Osama bin Ladin—who share with the suicide hijackers a hatred of the United States and the desire, ultimately, to transform it into a nation living under the strictures of militant Islam. Although not responsible for the atrocities in September, they harbor designs for this country that warrant urgent and serious attention. . . .

The Goals of Islamism

The ambition to take over the United States is hardly a new one. The first missionaries for militant Islam, or Islamism, who arrived here from abroad in the 1920's, unblushingly declared, "Our plan is, we are going to conquer America." The audacity of such statements hardly went unnoticed at the

1. the terrorist attacks against New York and Washington, D.C., on September 11, 2001

time, including by Christians who cherished their own missionizing hopes. As a 1922 newspaper commentary put it:

> To the millions of American Christians who have so long looked eagerly forward to the time the cross shall be supreme in every land and the people of the whole world shall have become the followers of Christ, the plan to win this continent to the path of the "infidel Turk" will seem a thing unbelievable. But there is no doubt about its being pressed with all the fanatical zeal for which the Mohammedans are noted.

But it is in recent decades, as the Muslim population in the country has increased significantly in size, social standing, and influence, and as Islamism has made its presence widely felt on the international scene, that this "fanatical zeal" has truly come into its own. A catalyzing figure in the story is the late Ismail Al-Faruqi, a Palestinian immigrant who founded the International Institute of Islamic Thought and taught for many years at Temple University in Philadelphia. Rightly called "a pioneer in the development of Islamic studies in America," he was also the first contemporary theorist of a United States made Muslim. "Nothing could be greater," Al-Faruqi wrote in the early 1980's, "than this youthful, vigorous, and rich continent [of North America] turning away from its past evil and marching forward under the banner of *Allahu Akbar* [God is great]."

Al-Faruqi's hopes are today widely shared among educated Muslim leaders. Zaid Shakir, formerly the Muslim chaplain at Yale University, has stated that Muslims *cannot* accept the legitimacy of the American secular system, which "is against the orders and ordainments of Allah." To the contrary, "The orientation of the Qur'an pushes us in the exact opposite direction." To Ahmad Nawfal, a leader of the Jordanian Muslim Brethren who speaks frequently at American Muslim rallies, the United States has "no thought, no values, and no ideals"; if militant Muslims "stand up, with the ideology that we possess, it will be very easy for us to preside over this world." Masudul Alam Choudhury, a Canadian professor of business, writes matter-of-factly and enthusiastically about the "Islamization agenda in North America."

For a fuller exposition of this outlook, one can do no better than to turn to a 1989 book by Shamim A. Siddiqi, an influential commentator on American Muslim issues. Cryptically titled *Methodology of Dawah Ilallah in American Perspective* (more idiomatically rendered as "The Need to Convert Americans to Islam"), this 168-page study, published in Brooklyn, remains largely unavailable to general readers (neither amazon.com nor bookfinder.com listed it over a period of months) but is widely posted on Islamist websites, where it enjoys a faithful readership. In it, in prose that makes up in intensity and vividness for what it lacks in sophistication and polish, Siddiqi lays out both a detailed rationale and a concrete plan for Islamists to take over the United States and establish "Islamic rule" (*iqamat ad-din*).

Why America?

Why America? In Siddiqi's judgment, the need to assume control here is even more pressing than the need to sustain the revolution of the mullahs in Iran or to destroy Israel, for doing so will have a much greater positive impact on the future of Islam. America is central not for the reasons one might expect—its large population, its wealth, or the cultural influence it wields around the world—but on three other grounds.

The first has to do with Washington's role as the premier enemy of Islamism (or, possibly, of Islam itself). In Siddiqi's colorful language, whenever and wherever Muslims have moved toward establishing an Islamic state, the "treacherous hands of the secular West are always there . . . to bring about [their] defeat." Nor are Muslim rulers of any help, for they are "all in the pockets of the Western powers." If, therefore, Islam is ever going to attain its rightful place of dominance in the world, the "ideology of Islam [must] prevail over the mental horizon of the American people." The entire future of the Muslim world, Siddiqi concludes, "depends on how soon the Muslims of America are able to build up their own indigenous movement."

Secondly, America is central because establishing Islamism here would signal its final triumph over its only rival, that bundle of Christianity and liberalism which constitutes contemporary Western civilization. . . . And thirdly, and still more grandly, the infusion of the United States with Islamism would make for so powerful a combination of material success and spiritual truth that the establishment of "God's Kingdom" on earth would no longer be "a distant dream."

But this dream will not happen by itself. To American Muslims, writes Siddiqi, falls the paramount responsibility of bringing Islam to power in their country; and to this goal, Muslims must devote "all of their energies, talents, and resources." For this is how they will be assessed on judgment day: "Every Muslim living in the West will stand in the witness box in the mightiest court of Allah . . . in *Akhirah* [the last day] and give evidence that he fulfilled his responsibility, . . . that he left no stone unturned to bring the message of the Qur'an to every nook and corner of the country."

The Role of Violence

How this desired end is to be achieved is a question on which opinions differ in Siddiqi's world. Basically, the disagreement centers on the role of violence.

As has been made irrefutably clear . . . , there are indeed some, not just abroad but living among us, who see the United States as (in the phrase of Osama bin Ladin) an "enemy of Islam" that must be brought to its knees and destroyed. . . .

But there are several problems with the approach of revolutionary violence, even from the perspective of those who share its goal. The most obvious has to do with its impact on American society. Although attacks like the 1993 bombing or the suicide massacres of September 11 are intended to demoralize the American people, prompt civil unrest, and weaken the country politically, what they do instead is to bring Americans together in patriotism and purpose. Those who mastermind them, in the meantime, are often caught. . . .

Non-Violent Methods

For all these reasons, the non-violent way would seem to have a brighter future, and it is in fact the approach adopted by most Islamists. Not only is it legal, but it allows its enthusiasts to adopt a seemingly benign view of the United States, a country they mean to rescue rather than to destroy, and it dictates a strategy of working with Americans rather than against them. As a teacher at an Islamic school in Jersey City, near New York, explains, the "short-term goal is to introduce Islam. In the long term, we must save American society.". . . Practically speaking, there are two main prongs to the non-violent strategy. The first involves radically increasing the number of American Muslims, a project that on the face of it would not seem very promising. Islam, after all, is still an exotic growth in the United States, its adherents representing just 1 to 2 percent of the population and with exceedingly dim prospects of becoming anything like a majority. Islamists are not so unrealistic as to think that these numbers can be substantially altered any time soon by large-scale immigration (which is politically unfeasible and might anyway provoke a backlash) or by normal rates of reproduction. Hence they focus most of their efforts on conversion.

Major Muslim Population Centers in North America

(North America statistics based on IFANCA estimates)

Metropolitan Area	Population
Los Angeles	700,000
New York (tri state area)	600,000
Chicago	400,000
Detroit	400,000
Toronto, Canada	400,000
Houston	300,000
Washington, DC	300,000
Southern Florida	250,000
Dallas	200,000
Philadelphia	200,000
San Francisco	200,000
Minneapolis/St. Paul	100,000

IFANCA (Islamic Food and Nutrition Council of America), www.ifanca.org.

They do so not only as a matter of expediency but on principle. For Islamists, converting Americans is the central purpose of Muslim existence in the United States, the only possible justification for Muslims to live in an infidel land. In the view of Shamim Siddiqi, there is no choice in the matter—American Muslims are "ordained by Allah" to help replace evil with good, and otherwise "have no right even to breathe." "Wherever you came from," adds Siraj Wahaj, "you came . . . for one reason—for one reason only—to establish Allah's *din* [faith]."

This imperative, relentlessly propagated by authoritative figures and promoted by leading Islamist organizations like the Muslim Student Association, has been widely adopted by Muslim Americans at large. Many attest to the sense of responsibility that flows from being an "ambassador for Islam," and are ever mindful of the cardinal importance of winning new adherents. . . .

Creating an Islamic Environment

But if increasing numbers are necessary, they are also not sufficient. After all, whole countries—Turkey, Egypt, Algeria—have overwhelmingly Muslim populations, but Islamism is suppressed by their governments. From an Islamist point of view, indeed, the situation in Turkey is far *worse* than in the United States, for it is a more grievous thing to reject the divine message as interpreted by Islamists than merely to be ignorant of it. Therefore, in addition to building up Muslim numbers, Islamists must prepare the United States for their own brand of ideology. This means doing everything possible toward creating an Islamist environment and applying Islamic law. Activities under this heading fall into various categories.

Promoting Islamic rituals and customs in the public square. Islamists want secular authorities to permit students in public institutions, for example, to recite the *basmallah* (the formula "In the name of God, the Merciful, the Compassionate") in classroom exercises. They also want the right to broadcast over outdoor loudspeakers the five daily Islamic calls-to-prayer. Similarly, they have agitated for publicly maintained prayer facilities in such institutions as schools and airports.

Privileges for Islam. Islamists seek public financial support for Islamic schools, mosques, and other institutions. They also lobby for special quotas for Muslim immigrants, try to compel corporations to make special allowances for Muslim employees, and demand the formal inclusion of Muslims in affirmative-action plans.

Restricting or disallowing what others may do. Islamists want law-enforcement agencies to criminalize activities like drinking and gambling that are offensive to Islam. While seeking wide latitude for themselves, for instance when it comes to expressing disrespect for American national symbols, they would penalize expressions of disrespect for religious figures whom Islam deems holy, especially the prophet Muhammad; punish criticism of Islam, Islamism, or Islamists; and close down critical analysis of Islam.

Some of these aims have already been achieved. Others may seem relatively minor in and of themselves, implying no drastic alterations in existing American arrangements but rather only slight adjustments in our already expansive accommodation of social "diversity." Cumulatively, however, by whittling away at the existing order, they would change the country's whole way of life—making Islam a major public presence, ensuring that both the workplace and the educational system accommodate its dictates and strictures, adapting family customs to its code of conduct, winning it a privileged position in American life, and finally imposing its system of law. Steps along the way would include more radical and intrusive actions like prohibiting conversion *out* of Islam, criminalizing adultery, banning the consumption of pork, formalizing enhanced rights for Muslims at the expense of non-Muslims, and doing away with equality of the sexes.

A Muslim majority? Islamic law the law of the land? Even the most optimistic Islamists concede the task will not be easy. Just as Muhammad confronted die-hard opponents in pagan Mecca, writes Siddiqi, so pious Muslims in America will face opponents, led by the press cum media, the agents of capitalism, the champions of atheism (Godless creeds) and the [Christian] missionary zealots. Doing battle with them will demand focus, determination, and sacrifice.

And yet Siddiqi also thinks Muslims enjoy advantages undreamt of in Muhammad's day or in any other society than today's United States. For one thing, Americans are hungry for the Islamist message, which "pinpoints the shortcoming of capitalism, elaborates the fallacies of democracy, [and] exposes the devastating consequences of the liberal lifestyle." For another, the United States *permits* Islamists to pursue their political agenda in an entirely legal fashion and without ever challenging the existing order. Indeed, precisely because the Constitution guarantees complete government neutrality toward religion, the system can be used to further Islamist aims. Democratic means are at hand for developing an active and persistent lobby, cultivating politicians, and electing Muslim representatives. Nearly a million legal immigrants arrive in the country each year, plus many more through the long coastlines and porous land borders. The courts are an all-important resource, and have already proved their worth in winning concession after concession from American corporations and public authorities.

Even so, the road will not be completely smooth. A delicate point will be reached, in Siddiqi's mind, as society polarizes between Muslim and non-Muslim camps "in every walk of life." At that point, as the struggle between Truth and Error "acquires momentum and the tension increases along with it," the "Wrong Doers" are likely to take desperate steps to "eliminate the Islamic movement and its workers by force." But if Islamists tread cautiously to navigate this point, taking special care not to alienate the non-Muslim population, eventually there will follow what Siddiqi calls a general "Rush-to-Islam." It will then be only a matter of time before Muslims find themselves not just enfranchised but actually running the show. . . .

Examining the Organized Muslim Community

Whether and to what degree the community as a whole subscribes to the Islamist agenda are, of course, open questions. But what is not open to question is that, whatever the majority of Muslim Americans may believe, most of the *organized* Muslim community agrees with the Islamist goal—the goal, to say it once again, of building an Islamic state in America. To put it another way, the major Muslim organizations in this country are in the hands of extremists.

One who is not among them is Muhammad Hisham Kabbani of the relatively small Islamic Supreme Council of America. In Kabbani's reliable estimation, such "extremists" have "taken over 80 percent of the mosques" in the United States. And not just the mosques: schools, youth groups, community centers, political organizations, professional associations, and commercial enterprises also tend to share a militant outlook, hostile to the prevailing order in the United States and advocating its replacement with an Islamic one. . . .

That a significant movement in this country aspires to erode its bedrock social and legal arrangements, including the separation of church and state, and has even developed a roadmap toward that end, poses a unique dilemma, especially at this moment. Every responsible public official, and every American of good faith, is bent on drawing a broad distinction between terrorists operating in the name of Islam and ordinary Muslim "moms and dads." It is a true and valid distinction, but it goes much too far, and if adhered to as a guideline for policy it will cripple the effort that must be undertaken to preserve our institutions.

What such an effort would look like is a subject unto itself, but at a minimum it would have to entail the vigilant application of social and political pressure to ensure that Islam is not accorded special status of any kind in this country, the active recruitment of moderate Muslims in the fight against Islamic extremism, a keener monitoring of Muslim organizations with documented links to Islamist activity, including the support of terrorism, and the immediate reform of immigration procedures to prevent a further influx of visitors or residents with any hint of Islamist ideology. Wherever that seditious and totalitarian ideology has gained a foothold in the world, it has wrought havoc, and some societies it has brought to their knees. The preservation of our existing order can no longer be taken for granted; it needs to be fought for.

Periodical Bibliography

The following articles have been selected to supplement the diverse views presented in this chapter.

As'ad AbuKhalil
"The Future of Islam and the West: Clash of Civilization or Peaceful Coexistence? (Review)," *American Political Science Review*, March 1999.

Karima Diane Alavi
"Turning to the Islamic Faith: We American Muslims Are Still Reeling from the Fact That Our Faith Has Been Hijacked," *America*, March 4, 2002.

Scott Appleby
"The Fundamentalist Factor," *Lingua Franca*, November 2001.

Daniel Benjamin and Steven Simon
"A Place at the Table: To Reduce Alienation—and Militancy—Among Muslims, Europe Must Invite Them In," *Time*, December 16, 2002.

Economist
"Two Theories (Political Islam)," September 13, 2003.

Dale F. Eickelman
"Inside the Islamic Reformation," *Wilson Quarterly*, Winter 1998.

John L. Esposito
"Struggle in Islam," *Boston Review*, December 2001/January 2002.

Khaled Abou El Fadl
"The Place of Tolerance in Islam," *Boston Review*, December 2001/January 2002.

Francis Fukuyama
"Has History Started Again?" *Policy*, Winter 2002.

Clifford Geertz
"Which Way to Mecca?" *New York Review of Books*, June 12, 2003.

Leonard B. Guttman
"Can Islam Be Hijacked? The Threat of Bin Laden," *Midstream*, September/October 2002.

Giles Kepel
"Islamism Reconsidered," *Harvard International Review*, Summer 2000.

Stanley Kurtz
"Root Causes," *Policy Review*, April/May 2002.

Jane Lampman
"Muslim in America," *Christian Science Monitor*, January 10, 2002.

Mustafa Malik
"Islam in Europe: Quest for a Paradigm," *Middle East Policy*, June 2001.

Syed Kamran Mirza
"Why Critical Scrutiny of Islam Is an Utmost Necessity," *Free Inquiry*, Spring 2002.

Ralph Peters
"Rolling Back Radical Islam," *Parameters*, Autumn 2002.

Daniel Pipes
"It Matters What Kind of Islam Prevails," *Los Angeles Times*, July 22, 1999.

Glossary

Allah God.

Allahu Akbar "**Allah** is Most Great."

ayatollah A high-ranking religious leader among **Shia Muslims**.

burka A garment used by some Muslim women, which consists of a robe that conceals the head, face, and body, with a small piece of netting over the eyes.

chador The covering worn by women in Iran, consisting of a dark cloth that covers the head and body and conceals the figure.

Dar al-Harb Literally, "House of War"; the non-Muslim world that is deemed hostile to **Islam**.

Dar al-Islam Literally, "House of **Islam**"; the Islamic world.

Dawa Literally, "call"; signifies an invitation to join the faith of **Islam** or the spreading of the message of **Islam**.

faqih A legal expert in Islamic jurisprudence.

fatwa An interpretation of religious law issued by an authoritative scholar or leader.

fiqh Islamic jurisprudence.

hadith Traditions or sayings attributed to the prophet Muhammad in the writings of his contemporaries and referred to for authoritative precedent in interpreting the **Koran**.

hajj The pilgrimage to Mecca that is one of the pillars of the Islamic faith; all who are able are required to make the pilgrimage at least once in their lifetime.

hijab A veil that fully covers the hair, or, more broadly, the modest dress that is required of Muslim women by the **sharia**.

huddud Literally, "limits"; the limits of acceptable behavior; the specific punishments designated under **sharia** for specific crimes, such as intoxication, theft, adultery, and apostasy (disavowing the faith).

ijma Consensus of opinion among the community or the **ulema**.

ijtihad Independent judgment on religious matters or principles of Islamic jurisprudence that are not specifically outlined in the **Koran**.

imam Religious or political leader, particularly among **Shia**.

Islam Submission to God and to God's message revealed to Muhammad; the religion of **Muslims**.

jihad Struggle; can be any struggle, from a personal striving to fulfill religious responsibilities to a holy war undertaken for the defense of **Islam**.

khalifah (often caliph) Literally, "successor" to Muhammad; the vice-regent or political leader of the Muslim state.

Koran (often Qur'an) Literally, "the recitation"; the text of Muhammad's revelations and prophecies; the holy book of the Islamic faith.

mujahideen (singular: **mujahid**) Persons who wage **jihad**.

mujtahid A person who exercises **ijtihad**.

Muslim A person who submits to God by following **Islam**.

niqab Garments worn by Muslim women that include a face covering and gloves.

pan-Arabism A movement seeking to unite the Arab nations of the Middle East and North Africa.

purdah A Persian word denoting the modest dress of women and the separation of women from men.

al-Sawa al-Islamia The "Islamic Awakening"; the term sometimes used to refer to the political **Islam** phenomenon.

sharia Literally, "the way"; the Islamic legal code as stipulated in the **Koran** and **hadith**.

Shia/Shiite Literally, "party" or "sect," specifically referring to the "party of Ali"; a **Muslim** who follows Ali (the cousin and fourth successor of Muhammad), who was deposed as leader of Muhammad's followers.

shura Consultation; the duty of a leader to seek the consultation of religious experts or the people.

Sunna/Sunni Literally, "path"; following the example of Muhammad set out in the **Koran** and **hadith**; refers to the majority Muslim denomination (as differentiated from **Shia**).

sura Chapter of the **Koran**.

ulema (singular: *alim*) Religious scholars, leaders, and experts.

ummah Community; specifically, the community of **Muslims**.

zina Illegal sexual intercourse, including fornication, adultery, rape, and prostitution.

For Further Discussion

Chapter 1

1. Hamza Yusuf argues that many arguments Westerners make about Islam are more revealing about the West than about Islam. After reading his article, and that of Roger Scruton, do you agree or disagree? Are his criticisms of the West relevant to the discussion of whether Islamic and Western values clash?

2. Yusuf argues that some critics of Islam hold beliefs and arguments similar to past anti-Semitic criticisms against Jews. At one point he compares Western depictions of Arabs with how Jews were portrayed by Nazis. Do you believe his analogy to be a valid one, or does it harm debate by unfairly denigrating critics of Islamic extremists? Defend your answer.

3. What basic differences does Roger Scruton cite in contrasting Islam and Christianity? After reading his and other viewpoints in this chapter, especially Enver Masud's, discuss whether or not you believe that theological differences between the two religions account for whatever conflict may exist between "Islam and the West," and comment on what other nonreligious factors, if any, may be involved.

4. Abdulwahab Alkebsi advances the pragmatic argument that since Muslims would never give up Islam in order to pursue democracy, the United States is better off trying to convince them that Islam and democracy are compatible if it wishes to promote democracy in Muslim nations. What are the strengths and limitations of this argument, in your view? Is it one that Robert Spencer addresses in his viewpoint? Explain.

5. Could Sajjad Khan and Robert Spencer be said to agree with each other on the incompatiblity of Islam and Western-style democracy, despite their differences of opinion on other matters? Explain your answer.

Chapter 2

1. Richard D. Connerney describes how his views on Islam changed after the September 11, 2001, terrorist attacks. Does such a personal description of evolving views make his conclusions more believable, in your view? Explain why or why not.

2. Connerney, Teresa Watanabe, and other authors in this chapter cite verses in the Koran in support of their respective positions. Why would such citations be important in arguments about Is-

lam? Are their differences of opinion the result of citing different verses of the Koran or of interpreting them differently, or both?

3. Javeed Akhter is a Muslim while John Perazzo is not. Is this status relevant in evaluating their arguments interpreting a fundamental Islamic concept such as jihad? Explain.

4. Patrick Lang draws a line between "ordinary Muslims" and Islamic fundamentalists. David F. Forte draws a line between Islamic fundamentalists and the terrorists behind the September 11 attacks. What evidence do these authors use to back up their respective distinctions? After reading these and other viewpoints, do you believe the September 11 terrorists "hijacked" Islam? Why or why not?

Chapter 3

1. Voula, an atheist, condemns not just Islam but also Christianity and Judaism for their "contempt of women." Does her strong antipathy toward all religion strengthen or mar her arguments against Islam, in your view? Explain.

2. What examples of women's rights granted to Muslim women do Mary Ali and Anjum Ali provide? Are there any important rights missing, in your view? If so, describe them.

3. Defenders of Islam, including Mary and Anjum Ali and Samana Siddiqui often argue that practices and ideas harmful to women are wrongly blamed on Islam and really stem from other factors, such as tribal culture. Do you think the arguments of Voula and Azam Kamguian, which are critical of Islam, take into account those secular factors? Defend your answer, citing examples from the viewpoints.

Chapter 4

1. Abdullahi Ahmed An-Na'im argues that the Islamic world should incorporate some Western values and reject others. Which values does he describe as worth keeping and which does he suggest are not? After reading his views and those of Muzaffar Iqbal and Ayaz Amir, do you think it is possible for Muslims to separate the good and bad in adopting Western values? Explain.

2. The Muslim authors in this chapter come from the Sudan (An-Na'im), Pakistan (Amir), Pakistan and Canada (Iqbal), and the United States (Nassef). After reading their articles, do you believe that knowing their national backgrounds helps you understand and evaluate their arguments? Explain why or why not.

3. Some American Muslims complain that they are victims of stereotyping—that other Americans assume that all or most Mus-

lims are dangerous religious fanatics with ideas that conflict with mainstream American values. Is there evidence of such use of stereotypes in the articles by Ahmed Nassef and Daniel Pipes? Or do the authors take steps to avoid stereotypes? Explain.

4. Daniel Pipes argues that some Muslims seek to change the United States into a Muslim nation. Describe this new Muslim nation in North America. Is it a place you would want to live in? Explain your answer.

Organizations to Contact

The editors have compiled the following list of organizations concerned with the issues debated in this book. The descriptions are derived from materials provided by the organizations. All have publications or information available for interested readers. The list was compiled on the date of publication of the present volume; names, addresses, and phone numbers may change. Be aware that many organizations take several weeks or longer to respond to inquiries, so allow as much time as possible.

American-Arab Anti-Discrimination Committee (ADC)
4201 Connecticut Ave. NW, Suite 300, Washington, DC 20008
(202) 244-2990 • fax: (202) 244-3196
e-mail: ADC@adc.org • Web site: www.adc.org

This organization fights anti-Arab stereotyping in the media and works to protect Arab Americans from discrimination and hate crimes. It publishes a bimonthly newsletter, the *Chronicle;* issue papers and special reports; community studies; legal, media, and educational guides; and action alerts.

American Muslim Council (AMC)
1212 New York Ave. NW, Suite 400, Washington, DC 20005
(202) 789-2262 • fax: (202) 789-2550
e-mail: amc@amconline.org • Web site: www.amconline.org

This nonprofit organization was established to identify and oppose discrimination against Muslims and other minorities and to raise the level of social and political awareness and involvement of Muslims in the United States. It publishes the monthly newsletter *AMC Report* and numerous pamphlets and monographs.

AMIDEAST
1730 M St. NW, Suite 1100, Washington, DC 20036-4505
(202) 776-9600 • fax: (202) 776-7000
e-mail: inquiries@amideast.org • Web site: www.amideast.org

AMIDEAST promotes understanding and cooperation between Americans and the people of the Middle East and North Africa through education and development programs. It publishes a number of books for all age groups, including *Islam: A Primer.*

Arab World and Islamic Resources and School Services (AWAIR)

2137 Rose St., Berkeley, CA 94709
(510) 704-0517
e-mail: awair@igc.apc.org
Web site: www.telegraphave.com/gui/awairproductinfo.html

AWAIR provides materials and services for teaching about Arabs and Islam for precollege-level educators. It publishes many books and videos, including *The Arab World Notebook*, *Middle Eastern Muslim Women Speak*, and *Islam*.

Canadian Islamic Congress (CIC)

420 Erb St. West, Suite 424, Waterloo, ON N2L 6K6 Canada
(519) 746-1242 • fax: (519) 746-2929
Web site: www.cicnow.com

CIC's stated goals are to establish a national Canadian network of Muslim individuals and organizations, to act in matters affecting the rights and welfare of Canadian Muslims, and to present the interests of Canadian Muslims to Canadian governments, political parties, media, and other organizations. Its publications include research reports examining the coverage of Islam in the Canadian media and articles including "Islam and Canadian Muslims—a Very Short Introduction."

Council on American-Islamic Relations (CAIR)

453 New Jersey Ave. SE, Washington, DC 20003
(202) 488-8787 • fax: (202) 488-0833
e-mail: cair@cair-net.org • Web site: www.cair-net.org

CAIR is a nonprofit membership organization that presents an Islamic perspective to public policy issues and challenges the misrepresentation of Islam and Muslims. It fights discrimination against Muslims in America and lobbies political leaders on issues related to Islam. Its publications include the quarterly newsletter *CAIR News*, reports on Muslim civil rights issues, and periodic action alerts.

International Institute of Islamic Thought (IIIT)

PO Box 669, Herndon, VA 20172
(703) 471-1133 • fax: (703) 471-3922
e-mail: iiit@iiit.org • Web site: www.iiit.org

This nonprofit academic research facility promotes and coordinates research and related activities in Islamic philosophy, the humanities, and the social sciences. It publishes numerous books in both Arabic and English as well as the quarterly *American Journal of Islamic Social Science* and the *Muslim World Book Review*.

Islamic Circle of North America (ICNA)
166-26 89th Ave., Jamaica, NY 11432
(718) 658-1199 • fax: (718) 658-1255
e-mail: info@icna.org • Web site: www.icna.org

ICNA works to propagate Islam as a way of life and to establish an Islamic system in North America. It maintains a charitable relief organization and publishes numerous pamphlets in its *Islamic Da'wah* series as well as the monthly magazine, the *Message*.

Islamic Information Center of America (IICA)
PO Box 4052, Des Plaines, IL 60016
e-mail: iica1@attbi.com • Web site: www.iica.org

IICA is a nonprofit organization that provides information about Islam to Muslims, the general public, and the media. It publishes and distributes a number of pamphlets and a monthly newsletter, the *Invitation*.

Islamic Supreme Council of America (ISCA)
1400 Sixteenth St. NW, Rm. B112, Washington, DC 20036
(202) 939-3400 • fax: (202) 939-3410
e-mail: staff@islamicsupremecouncil.org
Web site: www.islamicsupremecouncil.org

The ISCA is a religious organization that promotes Islam in America both by providing practical solutions to American Muslims in integrating Islamic teachings with American culture and by teaching non-Muslims that Islam is a religion of moderation, peace, and tolerance. It strongly condemns Islamic extremists and all forms of terrorism. Its website includes statements, commentaries, and reports on terrorism, including *Usama bin Laden: A Legend Gone Wrong* and *Jihad: A Misunderstood Concept from Islam*.

Islamic Texts Society
22A Brooklands Ave., Cambridge CB2 2DQ, UK
+44 (0) 1223 314387 • fax: +44 (0) 1223 324342
USA (503) 280-8832
e-mail: mail@its.org.uk • Web site: www.its.org.uk

This organization publishes and sells English translations of works of importance to the faith and culture of Islam, with the aim of promoting a greater understanding of Islam. Among the titles it offers is *Understanding Islam and the Muslims*.

Middle East Media Research Institute (MEMRI)
PO Box 27837, Washington, DC 20038-7837
(202) 955-9070 • fax: (202) 955-9077
e-mail: memri@erols.com • Web site: www.memri.org

MEMRI translates and disseminates articles and commentaries from Middle East media sources and provides original research and analysis on the region. Its Jihad and Terrorism Studies Project monitors radical Islamist groups and individuals and their reactions to acts of terrorism around the world.

Middle East Policy Council (MEPC)
1730 M St. NW, Suite 512, Washington, DC 20036
(202) 296-6767 • fax: (202) 296-5791
e-mail: info@mepc.org • Web site: www.mepc.org

The purpose of this nonprofit organization is to contribute to an understanding of current issues in U.S. relations with countries of the Middle East. It publishes the quarterly journal *Middle East Policy* as well as special reports and books.

Middle East Studies Association
University of Arizona, 1643 E. Helen St., Tucson, AZ 85721
(520) 621-5850 • fax: (520) 626-9095
e-mail: mesana@u.arizona.edu
Web site: http://w3fp.arizona.edu/mesassoc

This professional academic association of scholars on the Middle East focuses particularly on the rise of Islam. It publishes the quarterly *International Journal of Middle East Studies* and runs a project for the evaluation of textbooks for coverage of the Middle East.

Muslim Public Affairs Council (MPAC)
3010 Wilshire Blvd., Suite 217, Los Angeles, CA 90010
(213) 383-3443 • fax: (213) 383-9674
e-mail: salam@mpac.org • Web site: www.mpac.org

MPAC is a nonprofit, public service agency that strives to disseminate accurate information about Muslims and achieve cooperation between various communities on the basis of shared values such as peace, justice, freedom, and dignity. It publishes and distributes a number of reports on issues of concern to the Muslim community, such as U.S. foreign relations and human rights policy, including *The Islamic Foundations of Patriotism*.

United Association for Studies and Research
PO Box 1210, Annandale, VA 22003-1210
(703) 750-9011 • fax: (703) 750-9010
e-mail: uasr@aol.com • Web site: www.uasr4islam.com

This nonprofit organization examines the causes of conflict in the Middle East and North Africa, the political trends that shape the region's future, and the relationship of the region to more technologically advanced nations. It publishes *Islam Under Siege* and *The Middle East: Politics and Development*, two series of occasional papers on current topics.

Washington Institute for Near East Policy
1828 L St. NW, Washington, DC 20036
(202) 452-0650 • fax: (202) 223-5364
e-mail: info@washingtoninstitute.org
Web site: www.washingtoninstitute.org

The institute is an independent, nonprofit research organization that provides information and analysis on the Middle East and U.S. policy in the region. It publishes numerous books, periodic monographs, and reports on regional politics, security, and economics, including *Hezbollah's Vision of the West, Hamas: The Fundamentalist Challenge to the PLO, Democracy and Arab Political Culture, Iran's Challenge to the West, Radical Middle East States and U.S. Policy*, and *Democracy in the Middle East: Defining the Challenge*.

Bibliography of Books

Akbar S. Ahmed — *Islam Today.* New York: I.B. Tauris, 2001.

Hamid Algar — *Wahhabism: A Critical Essay.* North Haledon, NJ: Islamic Publications International, 2002.

Tamin Ansary — *West of Kabul, East of New York: An Afghan-American Reflects on Islam and the West.* New York: Farrar, Straus, and Giroux, 2002.

Karen Armstrong — *Islam: A Short History.* New York: Modern Library, 2000.

Asma Barlas — *Believing Women in Islam: Unreading Patriarchal Interpretations of the Qur'an.* Austin: University of Texas Press, 2002.

Charles Clark — *Islam.* San Diego: Lucent Books, 2002.

Juan Cole — *Sacred Space and Holy War: The Politics, Culture, and History of Shi-ite Islam.* New York: I.B. Tauris, 2002.

Hastings Donnan — *Interpreting Islam.* London, UK: Sage, 2002.

John L. Esposito — *Unholy War: Terror in the Name of Islam.* New York: Oxford University Press, 2002.

John L. Esposito — *What Everyone Needs to Know About Islam.* New York: Oxford University Press, 2002.

John L. Esposito and John O. Voll — *Makers of Contemporary Islam.* New York: Oxford University Press, 2001.

Khaled Abou El Fadl et al. — *The Place of Tolerance in Islam.* Boston: Beacon, 2002.

Matthew S. Gordon — *Islam.* New York: Oxford University Press, 2002.

Yvonne Yazbeck Haddad, ed. — *Muslims in the West: From Sojourners to Citizens.* New York: Oxford University Press, 2002.

Yvonne Yazbeck Haddad and John L. Esposito, eds. — *Islam, Gender, and Social Change.* New York: Oxford University Press, 1998.

Asama Gul Hasan — *American Muslims: The New Generation.* New York: Continuum, 2001.

Miriam Hoexter — *The Public Sphere in Muslim Societies.* Albany: State University of New York Press, 2002.

Muhammad Hashim Kamali — *Freedom, Equality, and Justice in Islam.* Cambridge, UK: Islamic Texts Society, 2002.

Gilles Kepel and Anthony Roberts — *Jihad: The Trail of Political Islam.* Cambridge, MA: Belknap, 2002.

197

Bernard Lewis	*The Crisis of Islam: Holy War and Unholy Terror.* New York: Modern Library, 2003.
Fatima Mernissi	*Islam and Democracy: Fear of the Modern World.* Cambridge, MA: Perseus, 2002.
John Miller and Aaron Kenedi	*Inside Islam.* New York: Marlowe, 2002.
John Francis Murphy	*Sword of Islam: Muslim Extremism from the Arab Conquests to the Attack on America.* New York: Prometheus, 2002.
Daniel Pipes	*Militant Islam Reaches America.* New York: W.W. Norton, 2003.
John Renard, ed.	*Windows on the House of Islam.* Berkeley and Los Angeles: University of California Press, 1998.
Malise Ruthven	*Islam in the World.* New York: Oxford University Press, 2000.
Edward Said	*Covering Islam: How the Media and the Experts Determine How We See the Rest of the World.* New York: Vintage Books, 1997.
Steven Schwartz	*The Two Faces of Islam.* New York: Doubleday, 2002.
Anthony Shadid	*Legacy of the Prophet: Despots, Democrats, and the New Politics of Islam.* Boulder, CO: Westview, 2002.
Jane I. Smith	*Islam in America.* New York: Columbia University Press, 1999.
Robert Spencer	*Islam Unveiled: Disturbing Questions About the World's Fastest Growing Faith.* San Francisco: Encounter Books, 2002.
Bassam Tibi	*Islam Between Culture and Politics.* New York: Palgrave, 2002.
Amina Wadud	*Qur'an and Woman: Rereading the Sacred Text from a Woman's Perspective.* New York: Oxford University Press, 1999.
Ibn Warraq	*Why I Am Not a Muslim.* New York: Prometheus, 2003.
Bat Ye'or	*Islam and Dhimmitude: Where Civilizations Collide.* Madison, NJ: Fairleigh Dickinson University Press, 2001.
Ravi K. Zacharias	*Light in the Shadow of Jihad.* Sisters, OR: Multnomah, 2002.

Index